Dr Peter Coleman is an author whose first book, *Weekends with Matt*, was published by Affirm Press in 2022. He has a PhD in cultural studies from Monash University. His primary reason for getting a PhD was to call himself 'Dr' on flights and get upgraded to business class. To date, no upgrade has been forthcoming. He works as a consultant in the not-for-profit sector, but can't be bothered explaining what that involves. His interests include the French philosopher Simone Weil and *Below Deck Down Under*. Peter has been married to his husband Mike for over 18 years. Their marriage has yet to lead to the downfall of society, but he still holds out hope.

AUSTRALIA'S MOST BIZARRE CRIMES

PETER COLEMAN

affirm press

affirm
press

First published by Affirm Press in 2024
Bunurong/Boon Wurrung Country
28 Thistlethwaite Street
South Melbourne VIC 3205
affirmpress.com.au

10 9 8 7 6 5 4 3 2 1

Affirm Press is located on the unceded land of the Bunurong/Boon Wurrung people of the Kulin Nation. Affirm Press pays respect to their Elders past and present.

A catalogue record for this book is available from the National Library of Australia

ISBN: 9781923046269 (paperback)

Cover design by Josh Durham/Design By Committee © Affirm Press
Typeset in 12/17 pt Garamond Premier Pro by Post Pre-press Group
Proudly printed and bound in Australia by the Opus Group

Dedicated to Denise,
who will be smiling in her mugshot.

INTRODUCTION

'Crime is terribly revealing. Try and vary your methods as you will, your tastes, your habits, your attitude of mind, and your soul is revealed by your actions.'

AGATHA CHRISTIE

A USTRALIANS LOVE TRUE CRIME. A 2022 study placed Australia as the top country in the world for investment in 'true crime entertainment'. Listening to podcasts about serial killers, murderers, cannibals and sociopaths has become a national pastime. As I'm writing this, the number-one Netflix series in Australia is a true crime docudrama. For a country of easygoing larrikins, we sure enjoy stories of bloodshed, betrayal and ruin.

Given one in five Australians is descended from convicts, it's perhaps unsurprising that we're intrigued by the criminal element lurking in our collective DNA. According to Brendan Kelly, Professor of Psychiatry at Dublin's Trinity College, people's obsession with true crime comes from a fascination with their own human nature: 'We are obsessed with the darker side of humanity. The bad things other people can do and the extent to which, maybe, we could do these things too if we had different circumstances or maybe life had been different to us.'

True crime teaches us that humans can be horrible. But we can also be annoying, creative, courageous, dramatic, dishonest, dimwitted, hopeful, hypocritical, impulsive, ingenious, inventive, loving, noble, passionate, prejudiced, remorseful, selfish, self-sacrificing and weird – really weird. That's what this book is about.

Australia's Most Bizarre Crimes is a collection of quirky and ridiculous, scandalous and preposterous, sublime and humorous crimes from across the decades. You'll read about abducted garden gnomes, teddy bear beheadings, life-threatening hatpins, goldfield ghosts, fake poets, sex magic, egg assaults, stolen hair and a lawn-stealing Minion. You'll explore micronations, zoological specimens, the opening of the Sydney Harbour Bridge and 19th-century poop collection. You'll learn about a host of bizarre laws, which make it a crime to scoop up bird droppings, speak with pirates, fight a duel, crash a wedding and vacuum loudly at night. You'll also discover that the dumbest thing you've ever done (probably) pales in comparison with the monumentally stupid mishaps described in this book.

They say crime doesn't pay, but it can give you a good chuckle at someone else's expense. Enjoy!

BULL BALLS AND A BIG MANGO

AUSTRALIA IS A *BIG* place. It's the sixth-largest country on the planet and the only nation to span an entire continent. We're known for our big spiders, big personalities and Big W. Australia is also home to somewhere between 150 and 600 'Big Things', but there's no official count and numbers vary depending on what you class as a Big Thing.

Australia's love of Big Things began when the Big Banana was erected in Coffs Harbour in 1964 (although some say Adelaide's Big Scotsman was the nation's first Big Thing). The Big Banana was the brainchild of banana salesperson John Landi, who was inspired to create a giant replica banana after hearing about the Big Pineapple in Hawaii. The monument was constructed out of timber and concrete in less than three months. The 13-metre-long and 5-metre-high banana soon became a cultural icon. It inspired a banana-themed fun park featuring water slides, mini golf, laser tag and ice-skating. The Big Banana was named the 'most bizarre and grotesque tourist attraction in the world' in 1995 (a worthy title) and remains a must-see attraction for any visitors to the north coast of NSW.

The Big Banana also inspired a national love of making Big Things, including the Big Beer Can, the Big Boxing Crocodile (it looks exactly like it sounds), the Big Bogan, the Big Captain Cook, the Big Cockroach, the

3

Big Golden Guitar (in Tamworth, of course), the Golden Gumboot (not all Big Things have 'Big' in the title), the Giant Koala (some Big Things have 'Giant' in the title), the Big Lollipop (the world's largest freestanding lollipop), the Big Merino (the biggest Big Thing in Australia), the Big Owl (aka the 'Penis Owl' because of its phallic appearance when seen from behind), the Big Stubby (constructed out of 17,000 regular-sized stubbies), the Big Ugg Boot, the Big Western Rock Lobster (not to be confused with the Big Lobster) and the Big Wine Bottle ... to name a few.

Included in this monumental mix are the six Big Bull statues in Rockhampton, Queensland, which is known as the 'Beef Capital of Australia'. The Big Bulls were erected between 1978 and 2000, and the replicas were designed to represent the main breeds farmed in the region. There's the Braford Bull, the Santa Gertrudis Bull, the Droughtmaster Bull, the Romagnola Bull and *two* Brahman Bulls. One stands at the south-eastern entrance of the city and the other is on a median strip adjacent to the Red Hill Homemaker Centre. The statues were made with a keen eye for detail, right down to colouring and anatomy.

It's only natural Rockhampton's Big Bulls would have big balls. These larger-than-life imitation concrete testicles have drawn considerable attention over the years, and not just because of their ample size. Ever since the Big Bulls first graced the city, unidentified thieves have been making off with their gonads at night. Some residents point the blame at visitors, claiming no local would ever perform such heinous acts of vandalism. There are rumours of a website that lists the Big Bulls' family jewels as a 'top 20' souvenir for any visitor to Australia. (The existence of this website has never been verified.) It probably doesn't help that the Braford Big Bull stands directly across the street from a Liquorland. To add insult to injury, there are two campuses of Central Queensland University in Rockhampton. (What happens in O-Week stays in O-Week.)

For years, the Rockhampton City Council employed the services of a local tradesperson to make replacement replica reproductive organs.

But as one set of balls was replaced, another disappeared. The council eventually chose to take drastic action and installed metal rods to secure the nuts in place. This succeeded in slowing, but not stopping, the testicular theft rate. Where there's a will, there's a way (and some thieves aren't afraid of using power tools). Despite the council's best efforts, Rockhampton's Big Bulls continue to be the victims of clandestine criminal castrations. The mystery of the knocked-off knackers remains unsolved.

Another disappearance caught the public's eye when the Big Mango in Bowen, Queensland, went missing in February 2014. Staff at the Bowen Visitor Information Centre told media outlets that the three-storey-high replica mango had vanished from the concrete platform where it was first erected in 2002. CCTV footage showed an unmarked mobile crane approaching the 10-tonne replica tropical fruit in the early hours of the morning, helped along by workers in disguise. According to the Bowen Visitor Information Centre, there were tyre marks indicating the mango had been transported south, but there were no reports of it spotted on the Bruce Highway (which was surprising, because a gigantic mango careening down the road is kind of hard to miss).

Staff denied any knowledge of the apparent 'theft', but questions were raised when a PDF file of a media release was linked to an advertising agency. The agency claimed they were only helping in the search, but journalists were unconvinced. Their suspicions grew when a 'wanted' poster of the missing mango appeared on social media bearing the logo of a local radio station. Police also confirmed the $90,000 statue had never been reported stolen.

The case was cracked when a fast-food chain claimed responsibility for the 'theft'. The whole palaver was nothing more than a promotional stunt for a mango-flavoured sauce. The Big Mango had been safe and sound in the bushes behind the Bowen Visitor Information Centre the entire time.

The local icon was returned to its rightful spot, where it remained undisturbed until 2022 when an accounting software company pulled another stunt and replaced the Big Mango with an inflatable half-mango (resembling a mango cut in half with the seed still inside). The promotion was to draw attention to the fact that almost 50 per cent of invoices owed to Australian small businesses were paid late. The original mango was soon back in place, but I'm guessing it won't be long before another PR company steals it away again.

Maybe next time the dairy farmers of Rockhampton could collaborate with Bowen Tourism and transform the Big Mango into a Big Mango Smoothie. Or Queensland Health could wrap it in a giant condom to promote safe sex? How about bringing the Big Banana, the Big Mango, the Big Melon, the Big Orange(s), the Big Pineapple, the Big Strawberry and the Big Watermelon together in one spot to make a Big Fruit Salad?

In the land of Big Things and big dreams, anything is possible.

TRAM BOY

MELBOURNE IS FAMED FOR its hipster coffee, record-breaking lockdowns, erratic weather and electric trams. Electric trams have been a staple of the city's public transport system since 1906 and are still an easy way to get around. Melburnians love their trams. Sometimes a bit too much ...

On 17 April 2005, a 15-year-old boy snuck into the South Melbourne tram depot under the cover of night. The teenager was wearing a jacket that closely resembled the standard-issue tram driver uniform. He carried three sets of tram keys secured three weeks earlier. He boarded a low-floor Citadis tram, inserted the keys and took it for a ride – and the story of 'Tram Boy' was born.

Tram Boy drove the 28-tonne vehicle through Melbourne, picking up and dropping off passengers as he went. He even reversed at one point when he overshot a tram stop (no passenger left behind!). Officials later expressed amazement at Tram Boy's skill. He successfully used the brakes, crossed intersections and manually changed tracks without any formal training. For the most part, the passengers had no idea they were being chauffeured by a pubescent hijacker. Tram Boy was a tram-driving savant.

Forty minutes after leaving South Melbourne depot, everything ground to a halt. Literally. The electricity was shut off and the vehicle was surrounded by several police cars. Tram Boy was arrested at gunpoint, pushed against a seat and handcuffed. Passengers protested the rough treatment of their young driver. The joy ride was over.

At a national press conference, Detective Senior Constable Barry Hills (who was rocking an amazing walrus moustache) spoke fondly of Tram Boy: 'He's a nice lad, he's a good lad. I think his obsession just got the better of him.' Who can blame a young man for following his passion?

Senior Constable Hills didn't believe this act of grand theft tram would stop Tram Boy from pursuing his dreams later in life: 'He loves them and speaking to him, he enjoys watching trams but I believe that if he stays on the straight and narrow, then it's certainly not going to affect his future.'

Tram Boy was charged with nine offences and appeared before Melbourne Children's Court two months later. We don't know what became of him, but it's nice to think that Tram Boy is living a blissful existence at the helm of one of Melbourne's many trams. Whatever the outcome, Tram Boy remains a modern hero who will inspire latte-sipping Melburnians for generations to come.

BIZARRE LAW #1

Most of us agree that incest is a no-no. It's a one-way ticket to genetic abnormalities and awkward family dinners. Everyone knows it's illegal to marry parents, siblings or children (because it's gross). But marrying relatives isn't entirely off the menu. According to the *Marriage Act 1961* (Australia), it's legal to marry your first, second or third cousin. If you think that's weird, it's *also* legal to marry your aunt or uncle, niece or nephew. Think about that the next time you get a birthday card from your Auntie Joan ...

In a curious legal twist, the prohibition against marrying parents, siblings or children extends to adoptive family. Under the law, an adopted relative has the same status as a genetic relative. This makes it a crime to marry your adopted brother or sister, even if you didn't grow up together or only met as adults. Meanwhile, it's perfectly legal to marry your mother's or father's identical twin. (Don't worry if you just threw up in your mouth – we all did.)

FAECAL FELONIES

BEFORE THE ADVENT OF modern sewage, the toilet situation in Australian cities was less than ideal. Mid-to-late-19th-century city-dwellers would typically dispose of their poop by leaving it in a sanitary pan at the back of their homes. The contents were called 'night soil' and they were collected once a week by the 'nightmen', who had the crappy task of collecting the night soil and transporting it by horse-drawn wagon to manure depots on the outskirts of town. They worked at night to avoid exposing residents to the stench.

Unsurprisingly, the whole 'leaving a pan of poop at the back of your house to be picked up by a dude with a horse' wasn't the most hygienic waste disposal solution. At the time, diseases such as typhoid, cholera and dysentery ran rife. The problem was made worse when nightmen couldn't be effed taking their cargo to the manure depot and made unauthorised drop-offs. This created some legitimately shitty situations.

SHITTY SITUATION 1

On 3 April 1875, three nightmen – Edward Kinsella, Alfred Kingsford and John Raine – appeared before Melbourne's City Police Court on charges of polluting the Yarra River with night soil. Beechworth's *Ovens and Murray Advertiser* used strong language in describing the case:

> The filthy brutes, to save themselves trouble and expense, had formed a shallow reservoir for nightsoil on the bank of the river, and had then cut a race from the reservoir to the bank. Fifty-two loads had been emptied in this way.

Ew.

SHITTY SITUATION 2

On 30 May 1888, *The Herald* reported that Melbourne nightman William Patterson had appeared before court on night soil pollution charges:

> Constable Green stated that at 1 o'clock this morning he was on watch in the St. Kilda Road, when he observed the prisoner coming along with his night cart. He went towards the footpath, and then returned to the cart, and deliberately opened the door and allowed the foul contents of the cart to escape on the road.

Gross.

SHITTY SITUATION 3

On 15 April 1889, John Beck appeared before Caulfield Police Court on charges of 'spilling nightsoil on the public street within the bounds of the shire of Malvern'. *The Age* referred to the case as 'The Nightsoil Nuisance':

The evidence went to show that this was a most deliberate and filthy act on the part of the defendant. An eye witness named Richard Alexander said that ... he heard a night cart coming along High-street about 9 o'clock in the evening, and looking round saw it was in charge of [the] defendant. It was driven along Jordan-street out of High-street a short distance, when the accused deliberately let down the trap door, spilling the contents along the street and over a vacant piece of ground contiguous thereto.

Yuck.

SHITTY SITUATION 4

On 9 November 1900, a sanitary contractor was fined £5 at Camberwell Court for 'carrying on a business offensive to the public without consent of the council'. The arresting officer said that the contractor had set up sheds in Burwood that were used as a makeshift 'night soil depot':

On 11th October witness saw men emptying the pans out of the cart. There were also two men washing the pans, and there was a very offensive smell.

Barf.

The wide-scale implementation of water-borne sewage mostly fixed the problem of shit in the streets. But like a turd that won't flush, the issue was back in the news in 2018 when residents of Greenslopes, Brisbane, were plagued by a bowel-movement bandit known as the 'Brisbane Poo Jogger'.

SHITTY SITUATION 5

Like any serial offender, the Poo Jogger followed a set pattern of behaviour. (Cue the opening theme song of *NCIS*.) He would take a break from his early morning run, pop down the private path of a Greenslopes apartment block, do his business and be on his way. There was often used toilet paper left at the crime scene, indicating preparation and malice aforethought.

An alliance of Greenslopians resolved to catch the culprit. They set up a night camera to determine the timing of the early morning movements. Once the window of 'poop-portunity' was confirmed, a resident named Steve staged a stakeout. On the morning of Friday 11 May 2018, the Poo Jogger took his usual route down the private path, dropped his daks and started to defecate. Steve sprang from his hiding spot behind some shrubs and took candid pics of the offender mid-act.

'There's a red light which goes on before the camera's flash goes off,' Steve explained in an interview with *news.com.au*. 'He saw that and looked at me as the photograph was taken. Then he just said, "Hello". At that point I decided to walk away.' (Can't say I blame him.)

The photographs finally led to the identification of the culprit. The Brisbane Poo Jogger was 64-year-old Andrew [Redacted]: a pillar of the community, Brisbane City Council Board member and national quality manager for a chain of retirement villages. Images of the grey-haired gentleman caught with his pants down (literally) soon plastered the pages of newspapers everywhere. There was even a story featured in *The Washington Post* and #poojogger briefly trended on Twitter.

In June 2018 a spokesperson for Andrew's employer confirmed he had resigned from his position. The spokesperson said the organisation was 'distressed and disappointed at the alleged incidents'. (Understandable.)

The Poo Jogger was arraigned before Holland Park Magistrates Court where he was issued with an infringement notice and fined $378.

More importantly, the good people of Greenslopes were safe to walk the streets without fear of human faeces. The hard work of Steve and his allies had paid off. Power to the poo-ple!

BIZARRE LAW #2

Before you accept a Facebook invite from a one-eyed, peg-legged man with a parrot on his shoulder, it's worth knowing that Victorian law prohibits correspondence with pirates. Section 70C of the *Crimes Act 1958* (Vic) makes it illegal to knowingly do business with a pirate, supply a pirate with munitions (you'll have to find another home for that pile of cannonballs in the backyard), fit out a vessel to trade with a pirate or 'conspire or correspond' with a pirate. Contravention of this law can result in up to ten years in prison. Any Victorian wanting to catch up with their pirate BFF would be well advised to cross the Murray and share tales of the high seas at the South Wagga Bakery.

MEDIA HORE

I T WAS THE FIRST Tuesday of November 1997. Thousands of spectators in suits and pretty dresses were gathered at Flemington Racecourse for the Melbourne Cup – 'the race that stops a nation'.

The starting gates opened at 3pm. Might and Power took an early lead, with 1995 Cup winner Doriemus in hot pursuit. Punters watched in tense anticipation as Doriemus gained ground in the final leg. But then something strange happened. A slender, shirtless man with wild hair ran onto the track and spun around. Fortunately, nobody was hurt, and the race carried on regardless. But it was such a weird thing to do. Why would anyone run onto a track with 24 stampeding horses galloping as fast as they can?

Might and Power finished first, beating out Doriemus in a nailbiting photo finish. The race was a defining moment in the horse's illustrious career. Might and Power would go on to become the first reigning Melbourne Cup winner to win the Cox Plate since Phar Lap.

It was also a defining moment in the ignominious career of Peter Hore, Australia's premier 'serial pest'. Hore's interruption of the Melbourne Cup was the first of many interruptions to come. He would soon become a household name. Australians everywhere would watch in tense anticipation to see which public occasion he was going to crash next, like a real-life, deranged version of *Where's Wally?*

I honestly don't have the mental or emotional energy to outline the complete history of Hore's public disturbances. His CV is way too long. Instead, here are some selected highlights for you to enjoy:

- Hore ran onto the field during the 1997 Australia vs Iran World Cup Qualifier and pulled down the goal net. Play was suspended while the net was fixed. Prior to the interruption, Australia was up 2–0. The stunt apparently took the wind out of the Aussie team's sails. Iran levelled the match 2–2, qualifying them for the 1998 FIFA World Cup. Many blamed Hore for the loss.

- Hore burst into the chambers of South Australia's Parliament House while eulogies were being read for the former state governor Dame Roma Mitchell. He stripped his shirt off and made several difficult-to-decipher statements before being escorted off the premises.

- Hore disrupted the 2000 Sydney Olympics men's marathon by running onto Oxford Street carrying a didgeridoo. (Why he was carrying the didgeridoo or whether he can play the instrument remains a mystery.)

- Hore lunged at supermodel Sarah Murdoch while she was on the catwalk at a 2001 lingerie fashion show in Brisbane. Sarah escaped the encounter unharmed. Police successfully applied to have Hore remanded in custody until his hearing (making him unable to attend several upcoming, high-profile events in Queensland).

- Hore appeared at EnergyAustralia Stadium in Newcastle before the opening whistle of a Newcastle Knights vs Parramatta Eels rugby league match in 2006. (He had warned Knights captain Andrew Johns of his desire to kick-off the match beforehand.)

He entered the grounds riding a tricycle, carrying two cats in a basket. He picked up the ball and kicked it to Johns. Less than impressed, Johns threw the ball at Hore (but missed).

🏃 Hore interrupted the Cole Inquiry into the Australian Wheat Board kickbacks scandal in 2006. Hore introduced himself to the Royal Commission 'as a future Prime Minister of Australia'. He would later run as an independent candidate (under the name 'PM Howard') in the 2007 Federal election race against Kevin Rudd in the electorate of Griffith. He won a surprising 2264 votes.

After his unsuccessful bid against Prime Minister Rudd, Hore largely retired from public life, with a few notable exceptions, including interrupting another Knights vs Eels match in 2008 by running onto the pitch with a guitar case on his back and jumping onto Eels forward Fuifui Moimoi mid-tackle before being crash-tackled himself by Eels halfback Brett Finch. Memories of the 'serial pest' soon faded and event organisers everywhere began to taper off their anxiety medications.

But on 4 April 2014, Hore was back in the news again. Sporting ragged hair, a long beard and wearing a 'WTF' T-shirt, he created a kerfuffle at a hearing of the Independent Commission Against Corruption (ICAC) in Sydney. It took six staff to remove him, and a police constable was injured in the scuffle. He shouted 'I'm Peter Hore, serial pest' as he was led away.

Hore later claimed he had gone into the ICAC building to use the bathroom. He was fined $600 and put on a 12-month good behaviour bond. That must have been challenging. 'Good behaviour' never really was Peter's style.

BIZARRE LAW #3

Until the law was repealed in May 2021, it was an offence for Western Australians to transport more than 50 kilograms of potatoes unless they were a member or authorised agent of the Potato Marketing Corporation. Unauthorised transportation of 50 kilograms (or more) of potatoes could result in a $2000 fine for the first offence and a $5000 fine for any subsequent offence. Under Section 22 of the *Marketing of Potatoes Act 1946* (WA), potato inspectors could stop and search a person's vehicle if they suspected an excess of spuds.

We don't know why this law was originally put in place. Food security was something of an issue in 1946, so that may have played a part. Perhaps a powerful potato magnate was working behind the scenes? Either way, Western Australians are now free to pack their car with as many starchy carbs as they like.

BONDAGE, MACHETES AND EGGS

IT'S GREAT TO MIX things up in the bedroom. Who hasn't at least entertained the idea of playing around with handcuffs, a spanking paddle or a can of full-fat whipped cream? But sometimes things get out of hand and you end up needing a lawyer (or getting something removed in an emergency room).

In 2019 a man living in Goolgowi in western NSW (let's call him 'Fred') put out the call for gentlemen who might be interested in a spot of role-play. Fred was looking for fellas willing to break into his home, tie him up and rub a broom handle around his underwear. Standard stuff. Fred was happy to pay for the privilege. He would give $5000 to anyone who made it a 'really good' event.

Terence [Redacted] and another Sydney man (let's call him 'Stanley') were up for the job. They were booked to stage their break-in on 14 July. The daring duo, committed to scoring that sweet five grand, brought along machetes to drive home the 'realism' factor. This was Meryl Streep–level method acting.

Things went awry when they broke into the wrong house. The home's occupant (let's call him 'Bob') thought it was a friend who would often pop over for coffee. According to reports, Bob shouted: 'Bugger off, it's too early!' (Bob obviously had a candid relationship with his coffee buddy.)

Bob heard someone ask if his name was 'Fred'. Bob removed his sleep apnoea mask and went to investigate. He arrived in the lounge room to discover two machete-wielding men, ready for action. Bob explained that his name was *not* 'Fred'. It was 'Bob'. Embarrassed by the mix-up, Terence and Stanley apologised, shook Bob's hand and departed. Bob called the police.

Terence and Stanley finally reached the correct address. Fred noticed that one of them had a 'great big knife' in his pants. Machetes weren't part of his fantasy scenario, so he asked them to leave all deadly weapons in the car.

Fred was the consummate host. He prepared a breakfast of coffee, noodles, bacon and eggs. Tuckered out from his early morning hijinks, Terence retired to the couch for a nap. That's when the cops arrived. After they discovered machetes in the car, Terence was arrested. He was charged with entering a home with the intention of intimidation with an offensive weapon. Fred's session of bound-in-underwear-and-rubbed-with-a-broomstick fun had gone horribly wrong.

Fortunately for Terence, he was found not guilty. His attorney demonstrated that even though his client had broken into a home brandishing a machete, he had not done so with the 'intention of intimidation'. His intention was to bring pleasure and make money. An innocent mistake.

As for Fred, let's hope he's found a guy who can tie a good knot, handle a broom and knows how to use Google Maps.

CREATURE CRIMES

AUSTRALIA IS RENOWNED FOR its distinctive and fascinating wildlife. Granted, some foreigners find the country's fauna less than appealing. It's common to hear fearful Americans complain they would never venture Down Under because of the 'snakes and spiders', and it can be hard to convince an anxious American that most of us don't step over red-bellied black snakes on our way to work in the morning. But when it comes to furry friends such as koalas and wombats, almost everyone's a fan. Sadly, the nation's cute critters aren't always treated with the respect they deserve.

In August 2015, a four-year-old echidna named 'Piggie' was abducted from the Currumbin Wildlife Sanctuary on the Gold Coast. A 24-year-old man and an accomplice broke in on the evening of Saturday 1 August and stole away with the prickly monotreme. Piggie was dumped 44 hours later on the outskirts of the sanctuary, where she curled up and hid under a log. According to Currumbin Wildlife Sanctuary's senior veterinarian Dr Michael Pyne, echidnas 'are difficult to hold, difficult to feed and ... stinky', which probably explains Piggie's sudden return. The main culprit was arrested and charged on 4 August. Fortunately, Piggie escaped the ordeal in one piece. She was back to living her best echidna life in no time.

A similar crime was committed in 2012 when a penguin was stolen from Sea World on the Gold Coast. (What is it with people abducting wild animals on the Gold Coast?) Twenty-one-year-old Rhys [Redacted] and 20-year-old Keri [Redacted] were visiting from Wales on working holiday visas. After enjoying themselves at a beach party, the lads thought it would be a good idea to break into Sea World, let off a fire extinguisher in a shark enclosure, swim with dolphins and steal a seven-year-old fairy penguin named Dirk.

The dynamic duo awoke with hangovers and a penguin waddling around their apartment. They tried to care for Dirk by feeding him and keeping him wet, but penguin maintenance proved too much. The pair dropped the small sea bird off at a canal where they were spotted by onlookers and the police were called. The Welshmen were arrested, and Dirk was returned to Sea World unharmed. Rhys and Keri pled guilty to theft and were fined $1000 each.

In the name of balanced reporting, it's worth noting that Australian wildlife isn't always the 'victim' of a crime. Sometimes it's the 'criminal'. In 2017, a brushtail possum was filmed shoplifting in the nursery department of a Brisbane Bunnings. The creature was caught on camera busily chowing down on lettuce seedlings in the middle of the day. Possums are nocturnal animals, so onlookers were surprised to see such a bold-faced case of daylight robbery.

A staff member eventually encouraged the intruder to leave (Bunnings declined to press charges). Meanwhile, the recording of the crime went viral on Facebook. Viewers of the video seemed much more concerned with the welfare of the culprit than any damage done to the store's property. 'He must be soooo hungry,' wrote one commenter, 'to brave it and stay chomping down those little succulent greens where people can clearly see him, poor little munchkin.' Poor little munchkin indeed.

A similar (but more extreme) case of theft was perpetrated in Mooroolbark, Victoria, in 2023, when nursery owner Humphrey

Herington lost thousands of seedlings at the paws of a rogue koala. Humphrey had noticed seedlings were going missing overnight but wasn't sure who or what might be responsible. The mystery was solved when he arrived at work one morning to discover 'Claude the koala' sitting on a bench next to the seedlings, hugging a pole.

Humphrey safely removed the adorable menace by wrapping Claude in a towel and delivering him to a neighbour's paddock where he was released into a tree. Undeterred, Claude returned a couple of days later for a midnight meal. His illegal incursions were only stopped when Humphrey erected koala-proof fencing. It is estimated Claude's feasting cost the nursery $6000.

But the capers of Claude the koala and the Bunnings possum pale in comparison with the most celebrated Aussie animal crime of all – Rags the kangaroo bashing up Marty Monster on live children's television.

The year was 1987 and kids across the nation would jump out of bed on a Saturday morning to watch *The Early Bird Show*. The five-hour-long variety program was hosted by rock singer Daryl Cotton, TV personality Marie Van Maaren and Marty Monster (performed by a man in a furry yellow monster suit). Marty boasted a giant head, broad red lips, crooked teeth and a surprised expression – he was quite the looker!

The show took an unexpected turn one morning when Daryl, Marie and Marty were visited by a ginormous nine-year-old red kangaroo named 'Rags'. Daryl was interviewing Rags's handler when Marty approached (Marie was wisely standing at a safe distance). Perhaps troubled by Marty's unusual facial features, Rags proceeded to physically assault the monster. After throwing a few punches, Rags grabbed Marty's head and dragged him to the ground. Unsympathetic to the monster's plight, the audience burst out laughing. As Marty wrestled with the muscular marsupial, Daryl exclaimed: 'I now pronounce you Monster and Kangaroo!'

The handler intervened and freed Marty from the kangaroo's powerful grip. As he recovered from the attack, Marty staggered around in a daze. Daryl checked on the monster's welfare by asking, 'Do you know what day it is?' Meanwhile, the handler fed Rags a slice of bread to help soothe the savage marsupial.

Showing a blatant disregard for his own personal wellbeing, Marty approached Rags for a second round. True to form, the kangaroo punched Marty a couple of times before clutching his head. After disentangling the pair, the handler scolded Marty: 'Go and sit down ... you're only a troublemaker.'

It was clear that Rags was getting aggravated. After attempting to soothe the beast, the handler asked Marty to bring another slice of bread. Marty approached the kangaroo with the peace offering but Rags was having none of it. He punched Marty square in the middle of the face and the monster dropped to the floor. The audience was delighted.

The word 'iconic' doesn't even begin to describe this classic moment of Australian television. The clip was shown around the world and remains a landmark cultural event to this day.

MYTHIC PRECAUTIONS

From time immemorial, there have been reports of large, hairy, ape-like creatures roaming the world. The Tibetans have the Yeti, the Canadians have the Nuk-luk, the Americans have the Sasquatch and Australians have the Yowie. To date, no definitive evidence of their existence has been uncovered (photographs always tend to be conveniently blurry). Most card-carrying zoologists dismiss these creatures as nothing more than a joke. But for believers, they're no laughing matter.

In October 2020, a 46-year-old woman appeared before the Gympie Magistrates Court in Queensland. Helen [Redacted] pleaded guilty to charges of producing marijuana and possessing illegal weapons. On a search of her home in Cooloola Cove, police found knuckledusters, knives, tasers and an illegal laser pointer. According to the *Courier-Mail*, they also discovered 33 marijuana plants and a glass pipe Helen had used for smoking meth.

Helen's lawyer claimed the marijuana plants were for personal use. But what about the weapons? The explanation was simple: she had amassed them in case of a Yowie attack.

Indigenous mobs across the country describe upright, ape-like creatures wandering the Aussie outback. There are several names for them, including 'Yahoos' or 'Yowies'. Settler sightings of Yowies are said to date back to 1795, but the first documented accounts come from the mid-to-late 1800s. One of the earliest accounts was written by amateur naturalist Henry James McCooey in 1882, who supposedly spotted a Yowie on the coast between Batemans Bay and Ulladulla:

> I should think that if it were standing perfectly upright it would be nearly 5 feet high. It was tailless and covered with very long black hair ... Its eyes, which were small and restless, were partly hidden by matted hair that covered its head. The length of the fore legs or arms seemed to be strikingly out of proportion with the rest of its body ... On the whole it was a most uncouth and repulsive looking creature, evidently possessed of prodigious strength, and one which I should not care to come to close quarters with.

Helen shared the same concerns 138 years later. In fact, she was so concerned that she procured both a butterfly knife *and* a credit card knife. 'What would a credit card knife do against a Yowie?' asked Magistrate Chris Callaghan. Helen argued she needed the knife for protection when camping in the bush.

Magistrate Callaghan remained sceptical: 'They're mythical, aren't they? They don't exist. You're talking about a mythical character.' He said Helen would need a more 'reliable' reason for stockpiling weapons than defence against cryptids. But he wasn't entirely unsympathetic. He accepted the marijuana was for personal use and let her off with a fine of $800.

The ruling was a win for Helen. It was also a win for any innocent Yowie who might have encountered Helen and her portable armoury.

BIZARRE LAW #4

People have been trying to make it rain for millennia (and by 'making it rain' I mean water falling from the sky, not showering onlookers with cash). For thousands of years, humans relied on magical methods to get the job done. 'Rain dance' rituals were performed by Zuni Native Americans, Chinese shamans and Ethiopian tribal leaders. The Ancient Romans conducted aquaelicium ceremonies for the god Jupiter in times of drought and the Aztecs sacrificed children to the rain god Tlaloc.

As magic fell out of fashion, people searched for more scientific solutions. In 1946, an American chemist named Vincent J Schaefer began experimenting with 'cloud seeding'. The technique involved dropping silver iodide crystals or dry ice into clouds from aircraft (or shooting the clouds with rockets or cannons for a more dramatic effect). Cloud seeding was only effective under specific conditions and in certain locations. It was more of a light-shower success than a weather-control revolution.

It looks like Victorian legislators in the 60s may have overreacted to the risks posed by cloud seeding. Section 9 of the *Rain-making Control Act 1967* (Vic) made it illegal for Victorians to engage in 'rain-making' activities unless authorised to do so. Anyone found guilty of unauthorised cloud seeding could face a fine of $1000 or 12 months in prison. The law says nothing about rain dance rituals or aquaelicium ceremonies. As for human sacrifices to the rain god Tlaloc, that's probably best avoided no matter how dry your roses get.

FOLIE À DEUX

L EO TOLSTOY SAID: 'ALL happy families are alike; each unhappy
family is unhappy in its own way.' This seems particularly apt in the
2016 case of the Tromp family, which triggered an interstate manhunt,
sparked national interest and still has people scratching their heads to
this day.

According to newspaper reports, the Tromp family piled into their
silver Peugeot SUV on Monday 29 August 2016 and fled their home in
Silvan, Victoria. They were about to embark on the family road trip from
hell.

Packed into the car was 51-year-old father Mark Tromp, 53-year-old
mother Jacoba Tromp, 25-year-old son Mitchell, and two daughters,
29-year-old Riana and 22-year-old Ella. They didn't tell anyone where
they were going or the reason for their sudden departure. They left all
IDs, credit cards and bank cards at home, only bringing along a small
amount of cash. The intention was to seemingly go 'off the grid' as
almost all the family's mobile phones were left behind. Mitchell was the
only family member to keep his phone, but that was chucked out the car
window near Warburton. It was later found on the side of the road.

They covered 800 kilometres on the first day, finishing up in Bathurst,
NSW. We don't know if they played 'I spy' or listened to music or sat in

awkward silence during the drive. Whatever happened, Mitchell was less than impressed. At 7am the next morning, he did the proverbial mike-drop and walked away. The rest of the family went to the Jenolan Caves in the Blue Mountains. This is one Tromp family decision that actually makes sense – the caves are stunning and totally worth a visit!

But this sightseeing sojourn wasn't enough to keep daughters Riana and Ella onboard. They ditched Mum and Dad, broke into a car and drove south to the town of Goulburn. (I think anyone who's spent a couple of days trapped in a car with their folks can relate.) They reported their parents missing before parting ways at a petrol station.

We don't know exactly why the sisters separated. Apparently, Ella wanted to go home to feed her horses. Meanwhile, Riana climbed into the back of a utility vehicle and hid. She was soon discovered in a 'catatonic state' by the ute's owner, Keith. 'She did not know her name and had no idea where she was,' he told the *Goulburn Post*. 'She mostly sat and stared straight ahead. She was a well-dressed young woman and she offered to give me $50 for my trouble.' (It's nice to be nice, even when you're in an altered state of consciousness.) Keith took Riana to the hospital where she was placed in psychiatric care.

If you're feeling confused, strap in! Things only get weirder from here ...

Friends and associates said there was nothing out of the ordinary about the Tromps before this incident. They were described as 'pretty straight', hardworking country folk. They weren't the kind of family to commit crimes, take drugs or go on clandestine road trips. They weren't in debt, their businesses were successful and nobody had any cause to wish them harm. The Tromps were remarkably normal.

Ella arrived home on the evening of 30 August, greeted by cops and journalists. Mitchell landed the next morning. When asked, 'What the fuck?' (or words to that effect), the Tromp siblings didn't have much to say. There was general talk of their father fearing for his safety, but not much else. (I think that's fair – most people struggle to explain their parents' behaviour at the best of times.)

Cut to their parents, who had driven south to Wangaratta, Victoria, (for reasons unknown). It was here Mark and Jacoba split up (for reasons unknown). Jacoba made her way back to NSW (for reasons unknown). She was later discovered in an 'agitated state' in the town of Yass (for reasons unknown) and transferred to a hospital in Goulburn.

Meanwhile, Mark had a close encounter with a couple in Wangaratta. The pair were driving at night playing Pokémon Go (the 'it' game of 2016) when they found themselves tailgated by a silver Peugeot SUV. Eventually, the couple and the SUV pulled over. After a pause, Mark jumped out of his car, ran into the middle of the road, stared at the couple and disappeared into a nearby park.

I told you things got weirder ...

Police searched the park without success. There was speculation that Mark may have broken into a nearby motel and slept the night, but this was never confirmed. Finally, at 5.50pm on Saturday 3 September, Mark Tromp was discovered walking on the side of a road near Wangaratta Airport. Journalists soon caught footage of him in a police car, covering his face and giving the middle finger to onlookers.

On 4 September, Mitchell and Ella appeared before the media to thank the community for their support. They reassured the public that both parents were doing well, and Riana was on the mend. When asked again *why* this had all happened, the siblings remained vague. 'I still feel confused,' said Ella. 'I think our state of minds wasn't in the best place ... There's no one reason for it – it's bizarre.'

More than anything, they were happy and relieved to know their family was coming home.

The following day, Ella was charged with stealing a motor vehicle and possessing proceeds of a crime. These charges were later dropped, presumably on compassionate grounds. Charges against Riana were also dismissed under the *Mental Health Act 2014* (Vic). (Fair enough.)

Mark Tromp released a media statement on 6 September thanking the police and community. He apologised for the 'hurt and concern' his actions had caused and asked for understanding as they processed the events of the last week: 'More than anything, my family and I need time to recover and receive appropriate assistance, including mental health services. To this end, we request that media organisations respect our request for privacy.'

And that was that. No further criminal charges were placed, and the story was largely left alone. The family returned to their everyday lives and peace was restored to the town of Silvan. But the question remains: what the hell happened?

The generally accepted theory is the Tromps were suffering from a rare psychological condition called 'folie à deux' (literally meaning 'madness of two'). This condition is a form of 'mass hysteria' where two or more people exhibit paranoid and delusional thinking at the same time. It's almost exclusively seen in tight-knit families living in isolated circumstances, which the Tromps were. The sufferers reinforce each other's paranoia and get caught in a 'negative feedback loop', hyping each other up until the anxiety reaches a fever pitch.

It's thought that actor Randy Quaid and his wife Evi were suffering from a bad case of 'folie à deux' when they sought asylum from a conspiracy of assassins called 'the Hollywood Star Whackers' in 2010. The assassins had apparently killed Heath Ledger and David Carradine and were also targeting Lindsay Lohan and Britney Spears. No evidence of this group's existence has ever come to light.

But unlike Randy Quaid, the Tromps never wanted the celebrity attention they received in September 2016. As Riana Tromp told *Woman's Day*: 'We are all very embarrassed. We didn't want to be famous, that's for famous people.'

THE NHILL GNOME HEIST

ON 6 FEBRUARY 2022, a Nhill man was arrested for stealing over 150 garden gnomes, statues and ornaments.

Before the arrest, residents across the Wimmera region in western Victoria had reported the abduction of their friendly, bearded lawn dwellers. Nobody knew why this kept happening and police were baffled.

A similar crime spree had beset Sweden in December 2005. Twelve garden gnomes were taken by a group calling themselves the 'Garden Gnome Liberation Army'. In a letter claiming responsibility for the kidnappings, the organisation said it had freed the gnomes from captivity and reunited them with their families for the Christmas season. The gnomes were later found standing in a circle in a forest.

The motivations of the Nhill gnome thief were never made public. It's unclear if he was an operative for the Garden Gnome Liberation Army or another garden gnome emancipation movement.

The missing gnomes were found at the thief's residence (I can just imagine their pointy red hats sticking out of every nook and cranny). Wherever possible, the lawn ornaments were returned to their rightful owners. The gnomes of Wimmera remain safe ... for now.

SOMETHING FISHY

Smug mainlanders love to poke fun at the Apple Isle. Who hasn't heard the one about the 'two-headed Tasmanian'? Inbreeding and sexual deviance jokes must get *extremely* boring for residents of the southern state, who only want to be respected as the decent and upstanding Australians they are.

So, I doubt many Tasmanians were too pleased when the following story was made public.

On 1 February 2023, a Tasmanian couple were charged with bestiality and 'prohibited activities in a cemetery'. A 57-year-old woman and 54-year-old man were arrested after two videos of the pair engaging in illegal and unwholesome acts circulated on social media.

One video shows the couple having sex on the grave of Tasmanian landscape artist David Hammond Chapman, who passed away in 1983 and is buried at St Mark's Anglican Cemetery in Cressy. The couple's conversation would suggest they were unfamiliar with the artist's celebrated career. The man in the video simply refers to the monument as 'someone's' grave. 'It's a grave, babe,' he says. 'We're going to fuck on the grave, that's where it's at.' The woman replies, 'To the souls of the faithfully departed, may they rest in peace.' We can only wonder if the dialogue was scripted or improvised.

The other video depicts the man using a live trout to perform a sex act on the woman, inspiring viewers to nickname her the 'Tassie Trout Lady'. Ever the raconteur, the man is heard remarking 'that's how you catch a trout'. It was revealed that the woman had previously worked at a veterinary clinic in Hobart. The clinic was quick to clarify they no longer had *any* connection with their former employee.

Police encouraged social media users to immediately delete the videos as possession of the footage could result in criminal charges. As for the good people of Tasmania, they'll no doubt be subject to bad 'Trout Lady' jokes for years to come.

CREEPY CLOWNS AND
GOLDFIELD GHOSTS

I N 2016, THE WORLD lost many beloved celebrities, including Carrie
Fisher, Debbie Reynolds, Alexis Arquette, Patty Duke, Alan Rickman,
George Michael, Gene Wilder, David Bowie and Prince. As if the deaths
of Princess Leia, Willy Wonka and Ziggy Stardust weren't enough to
deal with, the world was also plagued by random people dressing up as
clowns and scaring the living crap out of everyone.

The creepy clown craze kicked off in North America in August
2016 and quickly spread. From Canada to Scotland, frightened citizens
shared footage of strangers wearing scary clown masks and terrorising
the neighbourhood. There were also reports of 'clown attacks'. A teenager in Varberg, Sweden sustained minor injuries after being stabbed
by a man in a clown mask. In Pennsylvania there was a reported clown
murder. You couldn't make this shit up.

Victorian police were on the front foot when the clown craze hit
Australian shores, posting a statement to Facebook on 7 October: 'Victoria
Police are aware of people who are parading in the public wearing clown
masks ... Any intimidating and threatening as well as anti-social behav-
iours will not be tolerated.' A few days later, police arrested a Moe man

wandering around a fast-food outlet in the early morning, dressed in a clown outfit and threatening a woman with an axe. Not okay.

This was not the first time Victorians had been tormented by pranksters in spooky costumes. Long before the creepy clown craze, there was 'ghost hoaxing'. In the late 1800s and early 1900s, it was not uncommon for residents of the Ballarat and Bendigo goldfields to be accosted by mischief-makers dressed up as ghosts.

One infamous ghost hoaxer was known as 'the Wizard Bombardier'. The prankster dressed in a white wizard's outfit and terrorised the people of Ballarat, like an unhinged Dumbledore back from the dead. The *Kilmore Free Press* reported on the 'Wizard's' nocturnal activities in 1882:

> An apparition, in figure a man and in antics a mischievous school boy, has from time to time visited this claim at midnight ... and entertained the men at the premises at the times of its visit by means of a brisk bombardment with rocks, and its own sudden and mysterious disappearance whenever chased.

Ghost hoaxing was something the residents of the region were forced to live with, like a bad dad joke told at *every single* family gathering. An article in the *Bendigo Advertiser* published on 12 September 1903 spoke to the ongoing nature of the phantom problem:

> Another ghost is appearing in Ballarat in the neighbourhood of the Woollen Mills. A figure clad in flowing white robes has during the past few evenings entered the yards of several residents in the locality, to the great alarm of women and children.

But ghost hoaxing wasn't confined to the Bendigo and Ballarat goldfields. On 3 August 1895, the Melbourne *Leader* expressed strong disapproval of a spurious spectre in the Victorian town of Horsham:

> Some idiotic practical joker, suited in orthodox ghost costume, has been seen on the outskirts of the town, where he succeeded in severely frightening several children and nervous women. The police have the 'ghost' boom in hand.

Ghost hoaxing was also seen in other parts of Australia. On 1 December 1881, *The Ballarat Star* reported the case of a ghostly prank gone awry in the Riverina region of NSW:

> A cruel practical joke is reported to have been played upon a youth who recently visited some country relations in the Wagga Wagga district. He was taken out opossum-shooting by some of his young friends, who had previously arranged that some of their number should climb a tree and personate a ghost by covering himself with a sheet. Suddenly the alarm was given, and the conspirators de-camped in feigned alarm, but soon recovering their courage, they persuaded their young guest to fire at the ghost, having previously taken the precaution to see that his gun was only loaded with powder. The ghost descending from the tree, approached the party, and so terrified the lad that he became insensible, and was fully six weeks before he regained his customary health.

The ghost hoax trend also manifested in WA. On 27 November 1898, the *Australian Sunday Times* reported the case of a sham spectre having a run-in with the disgruntled people of Cannington:

> Considerable alarm was experienced by timid residents of Cannington, near Perth, at the frequent appearance of what was called a ghost. A number of residents waylaid the apparition, who surrendered on being bailed up by a revolver. The costume consisted of a sheet, with eyelet

holes, and decorated with red paint and other elaboration. The residents decided not to hand him over to the police, but to administer a sound thrashing with a paling. This was accordingly done and the ghost set at liberty.

The 'timid residents of Cannington' obviously weren't that timid!

Then there's this remarkable poem that ran in the *Cessnock Express and Mining and Farming Representative* on 13 July 1907. It tells the story of a ghost hoaxer who seriously pissed off the residents of Congewai, NSW. The ode was penned by Steele Grey and titled 'The Congewai Ghost Knock Out':

> It's just twelve months ago
> Since the Ghost made a start
> To scare all the rustics
> Who live in this part.
> Now there's a report going about –
> And perhaps it is true –
> That our Ghost is knocked out
> By the spirits of Mt. View.
> Well it wouldn't take much
> To knock out the ghost,
> As he was only a sham
> From scratch to the post.
> We thought we had a Ghost
> Of the genuine brand, –
> An up-to-date spectre
> Majestic and grand.
> But to our disgust
> We found – by the Lord –
> That our Congewai Ghost

Was only a fraud.
What a nice state of mind
A man must be in
When he uses his mouth
For a kerosene tin.
It was really dog mean
To play such a trick,
They reckon he should have
Been ducked in the creek.
But there are some of his victims
I'd venture to bet,
Who will try to locate him
And raise his scalp yet.

(Don't ask me to explain what he means by 'uses his mouth for a kerosene tin'. Maybe it has something to do with fire-breathing or drinking ... or both.)

Ghost hoaxing faded out with the onset of the First World War (dressing up as ghosts probably wasn't as fun with all the actual death going on). As for the creepy clown craze, it was done and dusted after only three months. After Halloween 2016 there was a precipitous drop in creepy clown sightings around the world. Nobody knew exactly why the clowns had stopped, and nobody really cared. It was chalked up as one more 'bad thing' to happen in what many called 'the worst year ever'.

Then 2020 rolled around and we learned what a 'worst year ever' really looks like. Turns out creepy clowns weren't so scary after all!

Shout-out to David Waldron for his fantastic article: 'Playing the ghost: ghost hoaxing and supernaturalism in nineteenth-century Victoria'. Check it out!

BIZARRE LAW #5

They say cleanliness is next to godliness, but when your next-door neighbour turns on their vacuum at 6am on a Saturday, cleanliness is a gateway to hell. You can usually solve this problem with a friendly chat or a sternly worded note shoved under the door. But when diplomacy fails, Victorians have another option.

Under Section 48A of the *Environment Protection Act 1970* (Vic), it's an offence to create 'unreasonable noise' with a vacuum cleaner before 7am and after 10pm on a weekday or before 9am and after 10pm on a weekend or public holiday. The same rule also applies to swimming pools, spas or water pumps, except when used to fill a heater tank.

A 'residential noise enforcement officer' can determine whether the noise qualifies as 'unreasonable' or not. If it is, the council or police can direct the vacuumer to cease and desist for 72 hours. Failure to comply can result in a fine of up to $23,077.20, which is enough to make any Dyson-determined neat-freak put their spring cleaning on hold.

SYDNEY STONER STUNT

O N 20 APRIL, STONERS everywhere can raise their bongs in celebration of cannabis. This unofficial international psychoactive drug
festival is known as '420' or '4/20' (using the American date style of
placing the month before the day). It is thought to have started in the
1970s by a group of California high schoolers known as the 'Waldos'.
The teenagers would get together and share a spliff after school at
4.20pm. Legend has it that one of the Waldos became a roadie for
the Grateful Dead bassist Phil Lesh. At a show in Oakland in 1990,
flyers were distributed inviting fans to light up on 20 April at 4.20pm.
The flyer was reprinted in *High Times* magazine the following year.
One thing led to another and the tradition turned into a global
phenomenon.

It's important to remember that 420 isn't just about getting wasted
on Mary Jane (although that is a key part of the festivities). Advocates
also use the day to promote the legalisation of cannabis via civil dis-
obedience (think Gandhi, but totally baked). The main strategy is to get
a group of weed aficionados to illegally toke up in a public place. Every
year, multiple 420 events are held across Australia. Because the recrea-
tional use of cannabis is illegal everywhere (except the ACT) there are
plenty of location options.

On 20 April 2022, Australian cannabis activists Alec Zammitt and Will Stolk took their protests to the next level. In the grand tradition of protest artists such as Keith Haring, Kara Walker and Ai Weiwei, the pair projected images of giant marijuana leaves onto the Sydney Harbour Bridge and Sydney Opera House. They also projected '420' and the question 'Who Are We Hurting?' – a slogan for cannabis reform in NSW. (Though the public art likely outraged several straight-laced Sydneysiders, I hope it inspired a few to get fully loaded on king-sized spliffs.)

Police raided the duo's hotel suite and charged them under Section 9 (g) of the *Sydney Opera House Trust By-Law 2021* (NSW). This law prohibits displaying 'promotional material' on the Sydney Opera House and carries a maximum fine of $1100.

Zammitt and Stolk pled not guilty. They told Sydney journalist Paul Gregoire that their stunt was designed to create 'thrill and impact'. 'Protest marches don't have the same epic impact,' said Stolk. 'We like to make people laugh. We like to make people think, and this is a really good and effective way of causing social change.'

The duo was undeterred by their legal troubles and back in action on 20 April 2023. This time they were protesting the laws prohibiting medical marijuana patients from driving. Zammitt and Stolk decorated armoured military vehicles (including a full-fledged army tank) with pot stickers and the slogan 'Driving with THC shouldn't make you an enemy'. They drove their military motorcade over the Sydney Harbour Bridge and past the Sydney Opera House before dropping past media outlets to promote their cause. No criminal charges were laid for the marijuana motorcade.

UNHAPPY LITTLE VEGEMITE

AUSTRALIA HAD ITS FAIR share of prime ministers in the 2010s. As one leadership challenge followed another, the country's highest office was held by Kevin Rudd, Julia Gillard, Kevin Rudd (again), Tony Abbott, Malcolm Turnbull and Scott Morrison – all within the space of eight years. It felt like the nation was playing a boring and stupid game of Pokémon. Gotta catch 'em all!

It began when Julia Gillard ousted Kevin Rudd in June 2010. Rudd's popularity had waned since his election victory in 2007 and many in his party felt it was time for a change. Realising he was outnumbered, Rudd stepped down and Gillard was announced as the country's first female prime minister.

In February 2012, Rudd staged a leadership spill of his own. This challenge prompted Gillard to publicly comment on the former PM's leadership style. She told a press conference her predecessor 'had very difficult and very chaotic work patterns'. Deputy Prime Minister Wayne Swan pitched in, saying Rudd had wasted his time in office with 'dysfunctional decision-making and his deeply demeaning attitude towards other people'. Stephen Conroy MP accused Rudd of having 'contempt' for his colleagues, and the former attorney-general Nicola Roxon called him a 'bastard'.

But the drama didn't end there. Just a few days before Rudd's leadership challenge, a video titled 'Kevin Rudd is a Happy Little Vegemite' was anonymously posted on YouTube. The video was a series of outtakes from a recording Rudd made in September 2009 to honour the 60th anniversary of the Chinese Communist Party. The clip shows a disgruntled Rudd swearing, slamming the table and bemoaning the quality of his speech. (To be fair, the speech he was giving was in Mandarin, which isn't the easiest language.) Highlights from the clip include:

- 'Tell these dickheads in the embassy to just give me simple sentences ... this fucking language, it just complicates it so much!'
- 'Tell them to cancel this meeting at six o'clock, will you? I don't have the fucking patience.'
- 'Is this the fucking Chinese interpreter up there?'
- 'Just fucking hopeless.'
- 'I fucked up the last word.'

The video also shows Rudd sitting motionless, staring directly into the camera, resembling a *Thunderbirds* puppet. All in all, it wasn't a great look.

When asked about the footage, Rudd confessed a penchant for using colourful language. 'I've never pretended not to swear from time to time,' he confessed in an interview on *Sky News*. 'I wish I'd sweared less but that's just the truth of it.'

Rudd also questioned the timing of the video's release, pointing out that it was 'a little bit on the unusual side' that the video had been uploaded only days before his leadership challenge.

He had a point. It was almost as if someone had anticipated Rudd's leadership challenge and wanted to get ahead of the game. What better way to reinforce the 'Rudd sucks to work with' narrative than uploading a video of him swearing and slamming tables?

The Australian Federal Police were called in to investigate. Theft from the Department of the Prime Minister and Cabinet is a serious offence that can result in up to ten years in prison. The police determined the footage, which was recorded on video cassette, may have been stolen in the period following Rudd's resignation in June 2010. Anyone with a parliamentary pass could have pocketed the tape amid the hubbub of the handover. There was no shortage of suspects and no easy way to narrow down the list.

The video had been uploaded by a user calling themselves 'HappyVegemiteKR'. Police attempted to access the user's metadata in the hope of finding personal information, but Google (which owns YouTube) was having none of it. In the interests of protecting 'free expression', Google's lawyers indicated they would only release the data if they were compelled to do so by the United States Department of Justice. The police abandoned this line of enquiry because the evidence available didn't meet the appropriate US legal thresholds for 'probable cause'.

After 17 interviews with potential witnesses and hundreds of hours on the case, police called off the search. Whoever 'HappyVegemiteKR' was, they had gotten away with it. To make matters worse for Rudd, there was no way to get the video taken down. As of writing, it's still on YouTube and the channel has 209 subscribers.

Rudd lost the 2012 leadership challenge to Gillard (I'm sure the video didn't help). He was relegated to the backbenches until another leadership challenge was staged in June 2013. This time he won and was reinstated as prime minister. He held the office until the new government was sworn in after Labor lost the election.

There were probably a few f-bombs dropped in the Rudd household that evening ...

CURIOUS CASES

ANYONE WHO READS THE news online or uses social media (which is pretty much everyone) is forced to deal with a constant cavalcade of clickbait – apparent 'news stories' about US foreign policy that turn out to be ads for protein shakes, top five tips for planning your career according to the phases of the moon, how you can make $20 million a year by sleeping 18 hours a day or 'lose weight fast' by getting a kidney removed. This attention-seeking crap is an unavoidable part of our online experience.

But clickbait is nothing new. Newspapers have been using catchy headlines to grab readers' attention since the 1800s. As literacy rates improved and newspaper sales soared, media outlets employed sensationalism to secure their place in the market. This practice was known as 'yellow journalism' (which I'm happy to confirm was *not* a racist term) and became popularised through the efforts of rival American media magnates William Randolph Hearst and Joseph Pulitzer. Their papers famously employed a high level of drama in their competing coverage of the Cuban War of Independence (circa 1895–98). My top five headlines from this period are:

1. **CRISIS IS AT HAND** CABINET IN SESSION; GROWING BELIEF IN **SPANISH TREACHERY**
2. PEACE TREATY IS RATIFIED. **AWFUL SLAUGHTER**
3. **GREAT SEA VICTORY FOR AMERICA!** VENGEANCE FOR THE MAINE BEGUN! **SPAIN'S ASIATIC FLEET BURNED AND SUNK!**
4. **SPANISH** SHIPS ON **OUR COAST! DIED IN** FOLDS OF **OLD GLORY!**
5. **SPAIN GUILTY!** DESTROYED BY A FLOATING MINE.

Of course, not all old-school clickbait headlines were this sensationalised and obvious. Newspapers had more subtle strategies for engaging the reader's interest. A common form of clickbait found in late 19th and early 20th century Australian publications was the use of the term 'curious case' in headlines. It was a nifty tactic for piquing the reader's interest in the 'curiousness' of the case at hand. I read *a lot* of these so-called 'curious cases'. There are literally thousands in the archives. Most of them are just stories about random incidents (a stolen horse, a dispute over a maid, a drunk man at a train station) mixed in with a few horrible injuries, domestic violence cases, medical abnormalities and miscarriages of justice. But after hours of panning for crime story gold in a river of garbage, I found a few fabulous nuggets to share with you.

To start with, here's a remarkable story of furniture theft combined with occult practices and a dash of circus performance:

'A Curious Case.' *Evening News* (Sydney, NSW), 29 September 1884

In the City Police Court yesterday Henry Winters was charged with having stolen about £40 worth of furniture from his mother-in-law, Mrs. Shepherd. They lived together; but while Mrs. Shepherd was away Winters had some of the furniture sold in Davidson's auction mart. A lot of nonsense was imparted into the case by the prisoner's brother, who described himself as a sword swallower, contortionist, and horizontal bar performer, lately attached to Chiarini's Circus. He said that he and his brother were concealed in a cupboard while the mother-in-law was invoking spirits to answer her questions. The son-in-law, who is a ventriloquist, answered the questions, which related in a great measure to himself. The defence to the case was that Winters really owned the furniture. Mr. Call, P.M., said that the matter in dispute was not one for the court; and the prisoner was, therefore, discharged.

Then there's this report of a piano tuning scam running rife in late 19th-century Darlinghurst:

'A Curious Case.' *The Scone Advocate* (Scone, NSW), 7 March 1891
A case which will be of interest to country residents who are sufficiently fortunate, or unfortunate, as the case may be, to own, pianofortes, was tried in the Central Criminal Court, Darlinghurst, on the 24th instant, when G H. Wakefield was charged with forgery. It would seem that, Messrs. W. H. Paling and Co. (Limited), of Sydney, send tuners at frequent intervals to the country districts. It was stated that the firm had been seriously victimised by impostors whose custom it was to travel the country representing themselves as Messrs. Paling's employees, and to tune or pretend to tune the pianos of Messrs. Paling's customers, collect the fees and ... defraud the firm of certain considerable sums of money ... the prosecution hoped that a light sentence only would be passed, its only desire being to expose this system of fraud and false representation and to put a stop to it if possible. The accused – Wakefield – was found guilty, and sentenced to two-years' imprisonment with hard labour.

I don't know about you, but I wouldn't call two years in prison with hard labour a 'light sentence'.

Next up, we have the sad tale of a man who *really* wanted to go to jail:

'A CURIOUS CASE.' *The Brisbane Courier* (Brisbane, QLD), 21 December 1894

About a quarter-past 2 o'clock on Wednesday afternoon a man named Edward Bradbury went into the city watchhouse and asked Constable Marshall to lock him up. The constable told him that he could not lock him up as he was not charged with any offence, whereupon Bradbury said that if he was not taken in charge he would break a window or do something else so that he would have to be locked up. The constable again refused, whereupon Bradbury took a stone from his pocket and threw it at the window of the watch-house. Marshall then arrested the man for disorderly conduct, and put him in the cells. He appeared before Mr. P. Pinnock, P.M., at the Police Court yesterday, when he was charged with the above named offence. On being asked how he pleaded he said he was guilty, and said, 'I have taken this means to bring my case before the public.' Mr. Pinnock said he did not know what his case was, and advised the accused to give himself up if he wanted to have his case brought before the public. Sergeant Taylor: If he goes out he will probably do some harm. Bradbury: As soon as I go out I will break a window again. Mr. Pinnock said he would require him to enter into a bond, himself in £5, to be of good behaviour, whereupon the defendant repeated his threat that if he was not locked up he would break a window. Mr. Pinnock then ordered him to be taken downstairs until he (Mr. Pinnock) could find time to deal with him, and in the meantime instructed the police to have him charged with vagrancy.

The following report is super short and super gross:

'A CURIOUS CASE.' *Norseman Times* (Norseman, WA), 9 March 1898

Miss Baker has successfully sued Dr. Purchas in the Supreme Court for £500 for grafting more skin from her body than had been agreed upon. This curious case has excited much interest amongst the medical profession.

If it's any consolation, £500 is equivalent to over A$100,000. At least Miss Baker could afford some fancy outfits to cover up her missing skin.

Then we have this rather intriguing account of stolen opera glasses and a strange exchange:

'A CURIOUS CASE.' *The Age* (Melbourne, Vic), 20 July 1899

At Fitzroy yesterday, two youths named Richard Kelson and Edward Whiting were charged with stealing a pair of opera glasses, valued at 20 [shillings]. The glasses disappeared from the shop window of Messrs. Beckett Bros., dealers, Gertrude-street, between 6 and 6.30 p.m. on Saturday, and were sold by Kelson at 8 p.m. to H. Miller, proprietor of a merry go round, for 2 [shillings] and a swing on a swinging boat ...

Is 'a swing on a swinging boat' supposed to be code for something?

I nearly didn't include this next story. I'm scared of dentists, and what happened here is beyond traumatising. But it's also incredibly ridiculous, so it had to be included:

'A CURIOUS CASE.' *Newcastle Morning Herald and Miners' Advocate* (Newcastle, NSW), 28 June 1901

A case was decided in the Melbourne County Court recently in which

Isabella Christina Burlington Vassie sued Clement Haddon and William J. Christy, dentists, of Swanston-street, to recover damages for alleged unskillfulness in the extraction of teeth, and also for extracting more of her teeth than she authorised them to do. Plaintiff said she agreed to have seven teeth taken out, but when she recovered from the effects of the chloroform she found that 18 had gone; including the whole of her upper teeth ... The defence was that the teeth were all decayed, and that [the] plaintiff, on being told so, left the question of their extraction entirely 'In defendants' hands, but against this there was the evidence of several witnesses that plaintiff had 'beautiful front teeth.' Plaintiff claimed compensation to the amount of £90. The jury returned a verdict for £20.

If I was Isabella Christina Burlington Vassie, I would have been *pissed*. Twenty pounds only adds up to around A$3900, which would have covered the cost of replacement dentures, but hardly makes up for the psychological trauma. She should have sued for millions!

Meanwhile, I was much less 'triggered' (and much more amused) by the following case of dental work gone awry:

'A Curious Case.' *The Cumberland Argus and Fruitgrowers Advocate* (Parramatta, NSW), 29 March 1902
At the Law Courts a few days, ago, a married couple made an application highly original in character. They applied to the Courts to stop their teeth from aching. It would appear that some time ago husband and wife underwent an operation at the hands of a dental surgeon, and were provided with surgical apparatus to be kept in the mouth for a certain interval. The apparatus, however, fitted badly and produced severe pain. It would have been thought that the natural course to pursue would have been to discard the apparatus, but the good couple wished to claim for damages from the dentist, and they were legally

compelled to keep the apparatus – and the toothache as well – until experts had been able to estimate the damages. If the slightest alteration were made in the position of the apparatus the experts could not have carried out their work. On the other hand, it is far from pleasant to suffer from toothache, even if compelled to do so by the law. The parties consequently made an application to the effect that they could no longer remain in their present position, and that an expert should be appointed in order to carry out his examination immediately. The application was granted, and the couple may now spend their prospective damages in curing their neuralgia.

The next report is like a spy movie where a secret agent says a 'trigger word' and the main character suddenly remembers they're an undercover assassin with mad kung fu skills (except in this case it's a 19-year-old boy breaking into a butchery in Dubbo):

'A Curious Case.' *Goulburn Evening Penny Post* **(Goulburn, NSW), 6 August 1904**

Dubbo, Friday. – At the Quarter Sessions today, Judge Dooker, in sentencing a young man, who had pleaded guilty to breaking and entering Moore's butcher's shop, in Dubbo, said he had received a letter from the accused's father, in Sydney, in which he stated that he was responsible for the crime, inasmuch as he had hypnotised the prisoner some time ago, and suggested to him that he should steal something. His Honor said if the father really did this, he was liable to punishment, while, at the same time, it did not excuse the prisoner. He regretted that the prisoner, who was 19 years of age, was too old to be sent to a reformatory. However, he would be sentenced to six months' imprisonment in Goulburn Gaol, to be accorded separate treatment.

If you've ever woken up with a nagging feeling of regret after a big night out, spare a thought for this briefly bigamous couple:

'Curious Bigamy Case.' *The Gloucester Advocate* (Gloucester, NSW), 7 August 1909

At the Collingwood Court on Tuesday John Anderson, a farm laborer (32), was charged with having committed bigamy.

Mary Anderson, of 123 Park-street, Abbottsford, gave evidence that as Mary Keenan, she was married to accused on April 15th, 1897. She went to live in Dight-street. Accused remained with her for only two days, and she saw no more of him for two years. She was 24 years old at the time of the marriage. In consequence of certain information, she took out a warrant for his arrest.

To Mr. J. Brennan (who appeared for the defence): Witness now lived under the name of Anderson, with a man named Collis, whom she had known for 22 years. Accused had never done anything towards maintaining her.

Mary Ellen Anderson, living at Station street, Carlton, stated that her maiden name was Trudgen. She was married to accused on June 30, 1902, at Holt's Agency, in North Melbourne. Accused had represented himself as a single man.

Mr. Brennan: 'Is it not a fact that this man was drunk at the time you married him?'

'That is so.'

'What condition were you in?'

'I was under the influence.'

'Is it a fact that you parted from each other as soon as you got outside the place?'

'Yes, he went one way and I went another.'

'When did you discover that you had been married?'

'When I woke up next morning.'

Sub-Inspector Bennett: 'How did you make the discovery?'

'My marriage lines were by my side.'

Plain-clothes Constable M'Cann, deposed that he executed the warrant on July 19 Waterloo road, Collingwood. The accused on being told the charges said, 'That's me all right, I got married twice, but I was drunk both times.'

Fans of *Seinfeld* or *Curb Your Enthusiasm* will enjoy this account of a minor irritation escalating into a major confrontation:

'CURIOUS CASE.' *The Burrangong Argus* (**Burrangong, NSW**), **8 May 1912**

BATHURST, Friday. – A rather unexpected development took place in a case which came before the Bathurst Police Court on Friday. A young man named Louis Eustace Beard, a dentist's mechanic, was proceeded against by Nathaniel Wood, a refreshment room keeper; of William-street, on an information alleged that he maliciously damaged some sugar of less value than 1s, by mixing pepper with it. Mrs. Wood also gave evidence that she saw defendant who was at a table waiting for refreshments, shake some pepper into a basin of sugar, and Mr. Wood said that when he spoke to defendant about it, he did not make a denial. Mr. Wood also stated that Beard and his companion, Phillip Hogan, a hairdresser, were not sober at the time. Both Beard and Hogan, however, denied the allegation on oath, and said that not only were they perfectly sober, but that they did not interfere with the sugar in any way. Mr. Wood (recalled), said that the practice had been going on for several years, and he wanted to make an example of defendant. Mr. C. Jennings P.M., said that at the outset the case was only a minor matter, but it had turned out to be a very serious one ...

Finally, we have the most curious case of all. It's a tale that's so bizarre, so unbelievable and so hilarious it must be true!

'A Curious Case.' *Heyfield Herald* **(Heyfield, Vic), 5 December 1918**
A man in Charter's Towers has just been sued for the price of his own coffin under rather remarkable circumstances. It appears that [the] defendant in the action, a miner named King, had died, or made so successful an imitation that the doctor was deceived, and the undertaker called in. The latter tradesman measured up Mr King, and provided him with an elegant black-and-old-gold coffin, that fitted like a glove, and then [the] deceased got up from his defunct position and refused to wear the coffin. He took it back to the undertaker on his own back, and the righteously indignant undertaker promptly returned it and left it on King's doorstep, whereupon [the] deceased kicked it into the street, and it was seized upon by two boys, who put four wheels and two shafts on it, harnessed up a goat, and used the vehicle for carting wood. Then the undertaker sued to recover the price of one large dark coffin, with gold trimmings, and a doorplate with King's monogram and all his virtues inscribed upon it. The late lamented Mr King pleaded that the coffin was not his because he was not dead. No man, he said, could be held responsible for a coffin ordered by others in his name while he was in a trance and unable to defend himself. The court held that King was responsible, and he paid under protest and in a state of unspeakable disgust. Then he went in pursuit of his coffin, determined to keep it by him for future use, but the boys had used it so badly that it was no longer fit to contain a decent Christian who had a reasonable amount of self-respect. So King sued the boys' parents for £5 damages done to a black and gold coffin, and lost the case, it being contended that he abandoned his right and interest in the coffin when he threw it into the street.

It was a tough break for Mr King. He had nothing to show for all that time and money except a busted coffin. I suppose it's better than being dead. My question is: what happened to the goat?

A MAN DROVE A STOLEN CAR TO HIS COURT HEARING FOR STEALING A CAR

IN JULY 2019, A 34-year-old South Australian man drove a stolen car to court to face charges of stealing a car. He arrived at court in Adelaide accompanied by a 23-year-old woman. They were driving a blue Holden sedan that looked strangely similar to one reported stolen a week earlier. The police ran the plates and sure enough, it was a match! (I must admit, I worry for the cops in this case. Imagine how jaded you would feel discovering that someone had driven a stolen car to their own car theft court hearing. I'm not sure my faith in humanity could ever recover from such a blow.)

The pair were arrested and charged. The humour of the situation was not lost on Senior Constable Rebecca Stokes. 'He'd actually stolen a car and turned up to court to face charges of car theft,' she told *ABC News*. 'We're hoping that when his partner attends court next month she catches the bus and we just break this vicious cycle.'

THE WRONG RIDE

HITCHHIKING IS ALWAYS A roll of the dice. You never know who's going to pick you up or where the ride will end. The driver could be the love of your life or a serial killer (or both). You could spend the trip in air-conditioned comfort or cramped in a Pontiac Aztek next to a crying baby listening to Nickelback's *Greatest Hits*. When you hitchhike, fate is your travel agent.

I doubt this risk was too much of a concern for three male convicts who escaped from the Ivanhoe (Warakirri) Correctional Centre in western NSW on 26 July 2006. The trio had travelled nearly 300 kilometres south to the border town of Buronga and were probably grateful for any driver who would pick them up (Nickelback or not). The men were hitchhiking on the side of the road when a car pulled over. The only downside: it was an undercover cop driving an undercover police car. The officer knew there were three fugitives at large and noticed the men's prison-chic green clothing. He arrested the escapees and took them directly to Dareton Police Station.

'You never know what's lurking around the next corner,' Sergeant Stuart Young told *The Age*. 'Though you don't normally have them fall into your lap like that. He was just the right person in the right place at the right time.'

As Morpheus said in *The Matrix*: 'Fate, it seems, is not without a sense of irony.'

COME A CROPPER

NOBODY CAN TRIGGER US quite like our parents. As the saying goes, they know how to push our buttons because they're the ones who sewed them on. Of course, parent-child tensions don't usually result in arson, but sometimes they do.

On 5 July 2016, police were called to a property in Humpty Doo, NT. The officers were summoned by a man whose father had burnt down his prized crop of cannabis plants. The son was described as 'indignant and enraged'.

Police asked if the man understood that possession of cannabis was illegal. Duty Superintendent Louise Jorgensen wrote on a Facebook post: 'He seemed to believe that destruction of the [cannabis plants] ... was far worse than the possession in the first instance.'

The father had recently moved in with his son from interstate. It looks like their interpersonal dynamic needed some work. As any good family therapist will tell you, arson is never the answer. Nor should you call the cops on your dad over the destruction of your contraband crop.

The police chose not to press charges. 'The evidence has been destroyed,' said Superintendent Jorgensen. 'Along with his reputation.'

A SUCCULENT CHINESE MEAL

I T WAS THE ARREST that launched a thousand memes. On 11 October 1991, a heavy-set, grey-haired, moustachioed man (let's call him 'DM') was picked up by police at a Chinese restaurant in Sydney. The media was notified of the arrest beforehand and cameras were rolling as the cops escorted DM out of the restaurant. This is when Network Seven recorded one of the most iconic monologues in Australian history.

In case you're one of the rare individuals who hasn't seen the video, it begins with an argument between DM and one of the arresting officers.

'You just assured me that I could speak,' says DM with a theatrical flourish worthy of a Shakespearean trouper.

'Sit down inside the car,' instructs the plain-clothes officer. 'We're not assuring anything. You're under arrest.'

'I'm under what?!' exclaims DM. He grabs onto the car as the police attempt to manhandle him into the back seat. He turns to the cameras and announces: 'Gentlemen, this is democracy manifest!'

DM launches into a curious mix of conversation and narration – like a Greek chorus written by an unhinged genius.

'Have a look at the headlock here. See that chap over there? ... Get your hand off my penis! This is the bloke who got me on the penis before. Why did you do this to me? For what reason? What is the charge? Eating a meal? A succulent Chinese meal? Ooh, that's a nice headlock, sir. Ah yes, I see that you know your judo well.'

DM finally succumbs to the police and addresses an officer sitting in the car: 'And you, sir, are you waiting to receive my limp penis?' Finally, he bids the onlookers 'ta-ta and farewell'. End scene.

The so-called 'Democracy Manifest' video is 69 seconds of pure larrikin gold. It has been watched *millions* of times since it was uploaded on YouTube in 2009. It has also inspired a wealth of memes and spin-off products, including birthday cards, fridge magnets, mugs, notebooks, scented candles, stickers, tote bags and T-shirts. There's a wine labelled 'GET YOUR HANDS OFF MY PINOT' and an Australian racehorse named Democracy Manifest. In 2019, *The Guardian* named the video 'the pre-eminent Australian meme of the past 10 years', praising the clip for its 'longevity, international popularity and relevance'.

But who was DM and why was he arrested?

It was long believed that the star of the video was a Hungarian émigré and chess master named Paul Charles Dozsa. Dozsa gained notoriety in the 1980s as a 'restaurant dasher'. Before his death in 2003, he had allegedly racked up over 100 convictions for 'dining and dashing'. It was assumed that 'Democracy Manifest' was a recording of Dozsa being dragged away for failing to pay yet another restaurant bill.

But in 2020, it was revealed that DM was neither dead nor Dozsa. He was an Australian actor, painter and reformed criminal named Jack Karlson. Aussie punk rock band the Chats had somehow managed to track Karlson down in hopes he would re-create his famous scene in their music video 'Dine and Dash'. Karlson obliged and the internet exploded with excitement at the triumphant return of 'Mr Democracy Manifest'.

The details of Karlson's strange and colourful life are enough to fill an entire book. In fact, true crime author Mark Dapin has already written that book. It's called *Carnage: A succulent Chinese meal, Mr Rent-a-Kill and the Australian Manson Murders*. From the 1970s to the 1990s, Karlson was a notorious thief, a serial prison escapee and an extra in several classic Aussie TV series. He became close friends with convicted armed robber and award-winning playwright Jim McNeil when they shared a prison cell in Parramatta Gaol. Karlson inspired McNeil to write a play titled *The Old Familiar Juice* – a play that Karlson also starred in. During a stint in Long Bay Jail, he discovered a talent for painting, which he continued to pursue as a free man. When *LAD Bible* interviewed 78-year-old Karlson at his studio in regional Queensland in 2020, he said that painting was all he 'ever wanted to do'.

It's a story of crime and creativity.

But what about that fateful day in October 1991? According to Karlson, it was a case of mistaken identity. He told *LAD Bible* in 2021 that the police mistook him for 'a Hungarian who used to rob restaurants' and falsely accused him of using a stolen credit card to pay for his meal.

What about his performance for the cameras? Karlson explained that this was all part of a larger plan. 'I tried to pretend to be a lunatic to get to a lunatic asylum,' he said. 'They're easy to escape from ... I've done it a couple of times before.'

But a different version of events was told by academic and musician Dr Dean Biron, who also happened to be one of the arresting officers featured in 'Democracy Manifest'. In a piece published in *The Monthly* in June 2022, Biron described himself as 'playing [an] anonymous extra in the *Citizen Kane* of viral videos, trying to persuade Australia's very own Orson Welles to exit the stage in the midst of his greatest performance'. According to Biron, Karlson was arrested and charged that day with 19 counts of fraud and receiving stolen goods valued at $70,000. But Karlson was prematurely released from custody and promptly disappeared. 'He vanished,' wrote Biron, 'like Keyser Söze in *The Usual Suspects* but without the finesse – until decades later when he re-emerged, somehow scrubbed clean of that pesky past and ready to take possession of his 15 minutes.'

Whatever the truth, the circumstances of Karlson's arrest hardly matter now. The overwhelming cultural impact of the 'Democracy Manifest' video far outweighs any questions of historical accuracy. Who cares why Jack Karlson was arrested? We should simply be thankful that the words 'succulent Chinese meal' and 'get your hands off my penis!' have been emblazoned on the nation's psyche. May Karlson's immortal monologue continue to uplift and amuse Aussies for generations to come.

THE TELLTALE SELFIE

JANE AUSTEN SAID THAT 'vanity working on a weak head, produces every sort of mischief'. I'm sure the 18th-century author wasn't thinking about Queensland drug dealers when she wrote this, but her observation is surprisingly relevant to this story.

In February 2015, police officers at the Gold Coast's Rapid Action Patrol (RAP) taskforce received a tip-off about an alleged pot dealer. They raided the home of the accused man, who adamantly maintained his innocence. The officers discovered the man's phone and decided to take a look. On the phone, they discovered a video of the man taking a shirtless selfie in the mirror. He was flexing his muscles and rubbing his stomach. He was also standing next to an enormous stash of marijuana.

The colour rushed from the man's face and the cops burst out laughing. He was officially busted. 'Police will allege that he produced, for want of a better term, the majority of the evidence,' RAP boss Superintendent Jim Keogh told *news.com.au*. 'Produced, directed, starred in and then screened it.'

'It could only happen on the Gold Coast,' he added.

Jane Austen couldn't have said it better herself.

A THIEVISH DISPOSITION

I'M ONE OF THOSE people who loses all self-control the moment I walk into a bookstore. I inevitably walk away four books heavier and $140 lighter. My internal dialogue usually goes something like this:

Q: 'Have you read all the books you have at home?'

A: 'Not even close. My to-be-read pile could fill two bookcases.'

Q: 'So should you be spending more money on books?'

A: 'Yes. Absolutely. I *need* and *deserve* them.'

It turns out this is a timeless experience. On Wednesday 26 October 1898, *The Argus* (a daily Melbourne newspaper) reported a court case presided over by Magistrate Joseph Panton. A young dressmaker named Julia Neil was accused of stealing three books and a music portfolio. Police searched her Carlton home and discovered another book, apparently taken from a set of volumes, entitled *Expositions on the Apocalypse* (sounds like a real page-turner). Julia claimed the book had been given to her by someone who knew her interest in Christadelphian literature.

The scene of the crime was Cole's Book Arcade, Bourke Street Mall, Melbourne. Founded in 1883 by the eccentric bookseller EW Cole, it was the largest bookstore in the world, boasting an incredible two million titles. It was also what marketing execs today call an 'immersive customer experience'. Visitors entered the arcade through a bright rainbow arch that led them into a festival of books, live music, plants, talking birds, monkeys, sweets, toys, garden ornaments, funny pictures, optical illusions and funhouse mirrors. Cole encouraged people to visit when they needed some time out. 'No one has to buy,' said a sign in the store, 'you can read what you like.' It was celebrated as 'the Grandest Bookshop in the World' and visited by such literary greats as Rudyard Kipling and Mark Twain. When a government regulation that dictated early closing times for bookshops threatened to shut the store down in 1896, 30,000 people signed a petition to keep it open. Everybody loved Cole's Book Arcade.

Well, almost everybody. It's clear Magistrate Panton wasn't the biggest fan. He took exception to the fact that customers could 'wander about' and pick up books at their leisure. This might seem a strange criticism to modern bookshop-goers. Isn't that how all bookstores work? But at the time, most bookstores required customers to ask a staff member before they could look at a book. According to Magistrate Panton, the freedom offered at Cole's Book Arcade was *making* people steal books: 'Temptation is thrown in the way of people who really are not thieves,' he said at Julia Neil's hearing. 'This place makes more thieves than any institution in Melbourne.'

Talk about victim-blaming! EW Cole refused to take the accusation lying down. He sent a letter defending the book arcade to the editor of *The Argus*:

> Sir – on returning from another colony today, I was surprised and pained to read in your paper of Wednesday the words uttered by Mr Panton from the bench on Tuesday last, referring to the book arcade ... Mr Panton has a strong bias against the book arcade; he can see the worst, but not the best side. In the Public Library any person is allowed to go into the bays and handle the books alone. There is temptation for the dishonestly inclined, but will Mr Panton venture to call

the Public Library a thief-making establishment, because dishonest persons can easily steal there? The Public Library is a grand institution, and does far more good than harm, and so does the book arcade ... I deem the above a sufficient answer to Mr Panton's strictures against the books arcade. Yours, etc., E. W. Cole.

But the war of words didn't end there.

On 5 November 1898, Magistrate Panton was back in *The Argus* after presiding over another case of book theft. This time a young woman named Ellen Smith was accused of stealing several books from Cole's Book Arcade and attempting to sell them off at a newsagent in Richmond. She confessed to the crime, but her lawyer claimed there were 'mitigating circumstances': 'For the defence, Mr Rogers contended that the books were left open for everyone to take, and there was no supervision. His client pleaded guilty. She had no apparent reason for stealing the books, and did not know why she took them.'

Talk about poor impulse control! Of course, Magistrate Panton took the opportunity to throw more shade at the book arcade. He claimed his comments about the store represented the opinion of every magistrate in Melbourne. 'We regret that facilities are afforded by these narrow passages,' he said, referring to the arrangement of the bookshelves in the arcade. '[They] do not admit without obstruction all the immense traffic that passes through there.'

How were people supposed to *not* steal books when the bookstore made it *so* easy?

A couple of days later, Magistrate Panton resumed the hearing of Julia Neil. EW Cole sent along barrister Dr TP McInerney to ask Magistrate Panton to 'qualify' his statements about the book arcade. But the magistrate wouldn't budge. 'By the correspondence that has taken place on the subject,' he said. '[EW Cole] has had a very good advertisement gratis.' Apparently, Cole should have been grateful for the free publicity!

Dr McInerney insisted Cole's Book Arcade didn't turn people into thieves. If someone stole from the store, it was because they already had 'a thievish disposition'.

The magistrate answered by referring to a recent case of 'boys' stealing books from the arcade. 'These boys were not originally thieves,' he said. 'If you will refer to the record of conviction you will see that our remarks are borne out. That is quite enough.' He concluded by sentencing Julia Neil to a 5-pound fine or one week in prison. Case closed. Or was it?

An article published in *The Argus* six years later showcased Cole's ingenious solution for shutting up the mean-spirited magistrate. There had been a significant drop in the number of book thieves appearing before the bench since the Julia Neil hearing. The article explained why:

> Some years ago it was the practice to prosecute offenders, with the result that Mr Panton complained of the number of cases brought before him, and condemned the Book Arcade as a resort of thieves and pickpockets. Since then, though many cases of pilfering are detected, prosecutions rarely follow, unless the thief becomes defiant or is known to be a frequent offender.

How could Magistrate Panton complain about the number of shoplifters if Cole didn't report them? It was, as they say, a 'boss move'. EW Cole for the win!

FAKE FRIENDS

THEY SAY IT'S NOT what you know but who you know. The 'right person' can open more doors than a good education, glowing CV and oodles of talent combined. It's hard to imagine Sofia Coppola landing a role in *The Godfather Part III* if her father hadn't been the director. (I've seen blocks of two-by-four cedarwood with a bigger emotional range than her.) It's also difficult to believe that Ivanka Trump's husband Jared Kushner – who looks like a villain from the *Annabelle* franchise – could have become senior advisor to the president without a little help from his father-in-law.

Former flight attendant Dimitri [Redacted] understood the importance of a good connection. In the late 2000s, he was busy raising funds for his start-up record label Emporium Music. When Sydney investors came to his office to discuss the new venture, they would see photos of Dimitri hanging with some of the most famous and celebrated people in the world. According to newspaper reports, Dimitri was pictured with the Dalai Lama, Pope John Paul II, Queen Elizabeth II, Nelson Mandela, Bill Clinton, George W Bush, Mikhail Gorbachev, Lachlan Murdoch, James Packer, John Howard, Kevin Rudd, David Hasselhoff, Molly Meldrum and Sophie Monk. It was quite the posse.

But the photos weren't real – and neither was the record label. To play the role of a wealthy music executive, Dimitri had doctored the photos, created false business statements and hired expensive cars. He claimed Emporium Music was worth millions, but there was only $208 in the company bank account. He squandered the investments on luxury living and keeping the fraud afloat. In the end, Dimitri fleeced a whopping $8.5 million from unsuspecting investors.

In June 2009 the con was exposed and Dimitri was arrested. He appeared before court in September 2012 on 16 fraud charges. He pled guilty but claimed he was unfit to stand trial because he had a 'psychotic illness'. Before his court appearance, he had met with forensic neuropsychologist Dr Susan Pulman. Dimitri told her he was suffering from hallucinations, paranoia and hearing voices – the textbook symptoms of paranoid schizophrenia.

'He came in and said a few things that he thought somebody who was alleging to have this illness would say,' Dr Pulman explained in an interview with the *Twisted Minds* podcast. 'He looked at my computer and said, "Oh, there's not a camera in there, is there? Am I being recorded ... I'm worried I'm being followed".'

His performance was about as convincing as Sofia Coppola's. It didn't take long for Dr Pulman to see through the lies. She confirmed that Dimitri *did not* have paranoid schizophrenia. She instead diagnosed him with narcissistic personality disorder.

The judge deemed Dimitri fit to stand trial and he was sentenced to 12 years in prison. He was remanded to South Coast Correctional Centre at Nowra, which was quite the downgrade after all those fictional parties with David Hasselhoff and the Dalai Lama.

DANGEROUS HEADGEAR

On 6 December 1911, the following letter was published in *The Brisbane Courier* under the heading 'Dangerous Headgear' (warning: this letter has major Edwardian-era incel energy):

> Sir, – The habit of women fastening on their heads hats that are eight or ten sizes too large with long and dangerous pins should be brought to an end. Not very long ago one of the dangerous implements ran into a man's face, blood-poisoning set in and death ensued. A Minister of the Crown in Sydney in passing through a crowd was wounded by one of these pins. On relating this incident to a Brisbane damsel, she laughed and said 'It served him right, he should not have been in the crowd.' A smoker who expectorates on the side walk, whereby a woman's trailing dress may be soiled, is liable to a fine of £20, whereas women themselves may endanger life with impunity – I am sir, etc., P.G.

I bet you didn't expect to be reading about hatpins in early 20th-century Queensland, but here we are.

PG wasn't alone in complaining about the hazards of hatpins. He was one of many Australians concerned with the risks they posed to public safety. After all, hatpins were very pointy and up to five-and-a-half inches long. For readers uninitiated in Edwardian fashion history, hatpins were pushed into the crown of the hat, through a portion of hair and out the other side, thus securing the hat to the wearer's head. Hatpins were extremely useful for keeping hats secure on windy days, but they could do some real damage if they stabbed you in the wrong spot.

Hatpins were the hot-button issue of the day and cities around the country were introducing laws to restrict their use. A piece titled 'Hatpin Nuisance' was printed in the *Queensland Figaro* on 16 January 1913 and refers to the anti-hatpin laws introduced in Sydney. The article was a plea for similar laws to be introduced in Brisbane:

That hatpin campaign in Sydney has evoked some very righteous confusion of face among the women of flash fashion folly. It can be no joke to be stuck up by a policeman on the piece of pavement in George-street ... Brisbane should go for a similar process of lessening the woes and the risks of many, through the silliness of a few. It cannot be forgotten that in the strike, some long pin 'ladies' wreaked their wildcat vengeance on innocent horses, when the 'look out – move' was actively carried out. Such women would make dangerous spouses.

The author was likely referring to the Brisbane General Strike in 1912. It was here that the 73-year-old suffragette Emma Miller toppled Police Commissioner William Cahill. Cahill had ordered his officers to go after a gathering of 15,000 protestors, shouting: 'Give it to them lads! Into them.' Emma Miller was protesting with a group of women and girls when they were attacked by a contingent of police on Queen Street. Miller was arrested but refused to back down. She removed a hatpin and stabbed the rear of Cahill's horse. The horse threw the commissioner to the ground, leaving him with a lifelong limp.

Australia's hatpin hysteria died down with the onset of the First World War in 1914. The mass carnage of war put the dangers of hatpins into perspective. Fashions changed and the problem vanished with time.

As for Emma Miller, she continued to campaign for the rights of the oppressed and marginalised until her death in 1917. Unfortunately, she is best remembered for bringing down a police commissioner with a hatpin.

EXECUTIVE ERROR

AUSTRALIAN COLES EXECUTIVE AARON [Redacted] stole $1.9 million from his employer in early 2019. He used the money to pay for rented real estate and a BMW, and splurged $200,000 on luxury goods. (I suppose those eye-watering Coles profits have to be spent on something!)

So how did Aaron pull off this large-scale embezzlement? Did he create shell companies in tax havens to launder his ill-gotten gains? Did he deposit the funds in a Swiss Bank account via anonymous, offshore enterprises using advanced encryption technology? No, he set up and approved payments into accounts *in his name*. Granted, some of the funds were sent to the Australian Taxation Office, but they were then redirected to accounts *in his name*. I really can't stress this enough: the accounts had *his name* on them.

Aaron pled guilty to fraud charges at a County Court of Victoria hearing in June 2023. The court was told he had already repaid over $1.3 million to Coles.

Judge Duncan Allan described Aaron's actions as 'strangely unsophisticated, bizarre and inexplicable'. He pointed out that 'a year 12 student could have worked out where this money was going'. (I honestly think a year 9 student could have cracked the case.)

'Brazen, that's one word for it,' said Allan. 'The other word is incredibly stupid.' (That's two words, Your Honour.)

In October 2023, Aaron was sentenced to three years and six months in prison, but he was eligible for parole after 20 months. The judge chose a lenient sentence based on Aaron's difficult past and his excellent prospects for rehabilitation.

After all, who hasn't done something 'incredibly stupid' from time to time? Maybe not directly-embezzling-money-into-accounts-with-your-name-on-them stupid, but we all have bad days.

In the words of Albert Einstein: 'Two things are infinite: the universe and human stupidity, and I'm not sure about the universe.'

BIZARRE LAW #6

'**F**uck You' by CeeLo Green hit the Aussie charts in 2010. Green's song about a jilted lover giving a massive FU to their ex was a Motown-style anthem everyone could enjoy.

Victorians singing along to Green's expletive-ridden banger probably didn't know they were running the risk of a four-figure fine or even a stint in prison! Under Section 17 of the *Summary Offences Act 1966* (Vic), it is an offence for 'any person who in or near a public place or within the view or hearing of any person being or passing therein or thereon' to sing 'an obscene song or ballad'. Victorians found guilty on more than two occasions of singing an 'obscene' song can face fines of up to $4,807.75 or six months' imprisonment.

But who gets to decide what qualifies as 'obscene'? In my opinion, 'Rockstar' by Nickelback, 'Strawberry Kisses' by Nikki Webster and 'Miracles' by Insane Clown Posse are 'obscenely' bad, but does that mean I can dob in a Melburnian who's rocking out to this garbage on Swanston Street? Probably not (there is no justice in this world).

The legislation mentions 'an obscene song or ballad'. I assume this is referring to traditional Australian ballads with risqué lyrics and not pop ballads such as 'Stuck with U' by Ariana Grande and Justin Bieber. The legislation was likely intended to cover bawdy ballads such as the early 20th century hit 'The Bastard from the Bush'. Here are a couple of verses to give you a taste:

> May the pangs of windy spasms through your aching bowels dart,
> May you shit your bloody trousers, every time you try to fart,
> May you take a swig of piss, mistaking it for beer,
> May the Push you next impose on, toss you out on your bloody
> ear.
> May the itching piles torment you, may corns grow on your feet,
> May crabs as big as spiders attack your balls a treat.
> Then, when you're down and out, and a hopeless bloody wreck,
> May you slip back through your arsehole, and break your bloody
> neck.

In an age when anyone can access hardcore porn on their phones and a self-described 'pussy-grabber' can serve as president of the United States, why do Victorians need protection from rhyming verses about farts and testicle-attacking spiders? As someone who values creative expression, music and swearing, I really think this law needs to fuck off.

PROBLEMATIC PRANKS

I T'S IMPORTANT TO HAVE a sense of humour. It makes the vicissitudes of life more bearable. But there's always that jokester who doesn't know the difference between 'hilarious' and 'felonious'. It's all fun and games until someone commits a misdemeanour ...

Twenty-year-old Max Jalal and 18-year-old Arman Jalal learned a lesson in the art of practical jokes when they were taken into custody in February 2016. The Melbourne-based brothers were arrested after posting a prank video filmed with their younger brother for their YouTube channel 'Jalals'. The video featured one of the trio dressed in stereotypical ankle-length Arab clothing pointing a fake AK-47 out the window of a car and pretending to shoot at random pedestrians (the AK-47 was actually a gold hookah pipe decked out to look like a gas-operated assault rifle). Fake gunfire sound effects were also broadcast from the car stereo. People were terrified and ran away, which is the appropriate reaction when you think you're being shot at.

The Jalal brothers must have been chuffed when the video went viral on YouTube and received thousands of likes on Facebook. They were probably less chuffed when 30 counter-terrorism police raided their home and hauled them off to jail. They were charged with public nuisance, possessing a prohibited weapon and behaving in an offensive manner in a public place.

A media storm erupted. The brothers faced harsh criticism from several commentators who labelled the stunt 'moronic' and 'abhorrent'. The brothers explained they were trying to 'parody ISIS' and help people be less fearful. In an interview with *The Project's* Waleed Aly, they admitted the prank was 'pretty irresponsible' (which is certainly one way of putting it). The brothers also showed remorse in an interview with Karl Stefanovic on *Today*. 'We apologise if we offended anyone through the prank,' said Max. (As a rule, you shouldn't use the word 'if' in apologies. It detracts from your sincerity. There's a big difference between saying 'I'm sorry I slept with your wife' and 'I'm sorry if you felt offended when I slept with your wife.')

Police dropped the charges of public nuisance and possessing a prohibited weapon prior to Max and Arman's sentencing at Melbourne Magistrates Court on 27 May 2016. Magistrate Charlie Rozencwajg ordered the pair to make a public apology and gave the media permission to film the occasion.

'It's obvious in the past that we have not made the best of decisions,' Arman said in his statement. 'We plan on pursuing a career in entertainment with better choices and more responsibility.' (To be fair, 'more responsibility' than pretending to shoot people is still quite a low bar.)

Magistrate Rozencwajg placed Max and Arman on a 'diversion program' that required they be of good behaviour for six months. He criticised the brothers for creating 'angst, fear and division', but said they 'obviously had a successful future ahead of them'. (At the time of writing, the Jalals YouTube channel has 4.64 million followers, so I'd say the magistrate was spot on.)

The Age reported that one of the brothers 'asked the police prosecutor for a selfie. He was firmly refused. "'That's OK,' said the Jalal – he'd just photoshop him in later anyway.'"

Another incendiary hoax was pulled off in Brisbane on 21 July 2018. At around 9.25pm, 27-year-old Christopher [Redacted] ordered an Uber to a unit complex in Sherwood. The Uber driver was more than a little perturbed when Christopher proceeded to pile what looked like a blood-covered bag containing a dead body into the boot of the car. The driver freaked out (understandable) and fled the scene. He called the police, who launched a full-scale operation. The unit complex was cordoned off and specialist police were called in to investigate. Thirty thousand dollars worth of taxpayer money was spent by the time police realised it was a prank gone wrong.

Christopher told *Nine News* that 'it was just one of those pranks that went out of proportion'. He explained that the 'corpse' was 'just a bag of vegetables with some shoes in it'. (The blood was fake.) He was filming the hoax with his friend Timothy [Redacted] in the hopes of going viral on YouTube. He never expected things to escalate so dramatically. Christopher only realised the enormity of the situation when police arrived to arrest him at TAFE. 'I was like, this is serious,' he said. 'There's like 20 police officers coming.' (*Nine News* also shared a photo of Christopher doing push-ups, with the caption 'he was also keen to show off his push-ups'. It's great to see he has so many strings to his bow!)

Detective Superintendent Tony Fleming expressed concerns that YouTubers pretending to put dead bodies in Ubers wasn't beneficial for society. He worried such hijinks would create a 'boy who cried wolf environment' where reports of blood-stained body bags wouldn't be treated with the appropriate degree of seriousness. 'I get that some people might see this as funny,' said the superintendent. 'Self-evidently we don't and it's not that we don't have a sense of humour.' (Have you ever heard cops joking? It gets *dark*.)

Christopher and Timothy were charged with 'making a false representation by conduct resulting in a police investigation', which is police language for 'you wasted our goddamn time'.

More police time was wasted when a partner at a prominent commercial law firm pretended to be abducted on a flight from Sydney to Tasmania on 12 October 2023. Chris [Redacted] suffered a serious lapse in judgment when he went to the toilet and scribbled a note that reportedly said, 'I am being held against my will. Send help.' He tried to get the note to one of his colleagues, but a flight attendant intercepted it and alerted the authorities. Chris must have been feeling the heat when the plane landed and he saw the police and fire brigade ready for action. He was taken into custody while police investigated the imaginary abduction threat.

Fortunately for Chris, police let him off with a minor infringement notice. Unfortunately for Chris, he lost his job at the law firm. They couldn't see the funny side.

LOST PROPERTY

A POLICE STATION IS USUALLY the safest place to lose something, but this was not the case for a 52-year-old man who accidentally left his bag in the foyer of Windsor Police Station in north-west Sydney on 7 March 2016.

The man returned half an hour later to recover his property. But there was a hitch. The police had already searched the bag and were surprised to discover a bong and cannabis among the man's possessions. Police confiscated the bong and drugs. They also issued the man with a 'cannabis caution'. I'm sure he was much more cautious after that.

GUILTY UNDER DURESS

AUSTRALIANS FACED SIGNIFICANT RESTRICTIONS during the COVID-19 pandemic. Lockdowns made it illegal to have large social gatherings, leave the house unmasked or pop over to the Maldives for a quick vacay. It's not easy to lose basic freedoms and many people struggled to make sense of the situation. Granted, most of us resigned ourselves to sitting on the couch, cracking open a box of wine at 11am and rewatching episodes of *Tiger King*. But some Aussies chose to 'fight the system'. There were illegal gatherings, protest marches and *extremely* active Facebook groups. There was also an insignificant, unsuccessful plot to overthrow the Australian Government.

On 31 July 2021, police charged a 49-year-old Perth man, Marcus [Redacted], with impersonating a Commonwealth public official. This was one of several police crackdowns across the country to stop a small group of wannabe revolutionaries who had hatched a plan to 'arrest' high-level politicians and public servants before establishing themselves as the new leaders of the land. They had released an online video, apparently showing the Australian Federal Police (AFP) Commissioner Reece Kershaw calling for people to 'dissolve' the Federal Government (the video was fake). The group had also ordered 470 replica AFP badges, later found dumped in a creek in Cairns.

'We have found no evidence this group has the ability – or has actually attempted – to carry out specific violent acts in support of statements made by members of this group,' said AFP Assistant Commissioner of Counter-Terrorism Scott Lee. 'But the behaviour of these people is extremely concerning.' (You're not wrong, Scott.)

Forty-nine-year-old conspiracy theorist and right-wing political candidate Teresa Angela van Lieshout was also charged with impersonating a Commonwealth public official, as well as importing fake AFP badges from China. A one-time candidate for Pauline Hanson's One Nation Party, Teresa was endorsed as a representative of Clive Palmer's United Australia Party in 2013 but dumped after 12 days because she accused Clive of human trafficking (that kind of accusation can really spoil a working relationship). She ran for State and Federal Parliament several times but never received more than 1.8 per cent of the vote. She launched her 2014 campaign in the Vasse state by-election by releasing a video of her posing in a black bikini and holding a fishing rod. Sadly, her swimsuit stunt didn't convert into voters, and Teresa placed last.

Her history of chronic political failure may explain why, in the failed 'coup' of 2021, Teresa tried to upgrade her political position by impersonating the Governor-General of Australia. Talk about a glow-up!

Teresa appeared before Adelaide Magistrates Court on 14 September 2023 dressed in a 'Freedom Fighter 2020' T-shirt. When Magistrate Simon Smart asked for her plea, she answered: 'I plead guilty under duress, Your Honour.'

The magistrate wasn't having it. 'It's either a plea of guilty or not guilty,' he said. 'I simply need an answer, guilty or not guilty, okay?'

Teresa conferred with her lawyers for 15 minutes (I'm sure that was a thrilling conversation) and returned to the dock with a simple plea of 'guilty'.

In October 2023, Teresa was sentenced to two months in prison, backdated for time served. She was also fined $200, which seems quite reasonable compared to the punishments other insurgents have faced throughout history (beheading; firing squad; hanged, drawn and quartered). But Teresa wasn't satisfied. 'I'll be putting this in the book I'm writing,' she said as she left the court.

I guess that makes two of us.

DOLL DRAMA

I FOUND THIS QUOTE BY Mark Twain on Instagram: 'Nothing that grieves us can be called little: by the eternal laws of proportion a child's loss of a doll and a king's loss of a crown are events of the same size.' This insightful observation on the nature of human suffering inspired me to investigate instances of Australian doll theft (researching this book has really changed the way I look at things). I uncovered more than enough examples to fill a chapter, because the world is insane.

The following reports span a century. They give us a glimpse into shifting societal norms and changing approaches to reporting. More importantly, they describe people stealing dolls, which is so effed up it's interesting.

DOLL DRAMA 1

On 13 December 1926, a piece titled 'MAN WHO STOLE DOLL' ran in the Launceston *Examiner*:

> At the Hobart Police Court on Saturday morning Roy Crooks, a young man, was fined £5 for having stolen a doll valued at £5 from a shop in Liverpool-street, occupied by, Mrs. Susan Slevin. Crooks said that he was drunk at the time, and knew nothing of what he was doing.

The old 'I was black-out drunk when I stole the doll' excuse. A classic.

DOLL DRAMA 2

On 8 January 1931, the *Adelaide Observer* ran a story captioned 'STOLEN MAMA DOLL REPLACED BY NEW ONE'. It concerned 'little Gladys Miller' of Fitzroy, Melbourne, whose 'sleeping Ma Ma doll' was stolen by another little girl from the veranda of her home. Gladys wrote to *The Herald* newspaper on Christmas Eve pleading for the safe return of her doll. On Monday 5 January 1931, *The Herald* published this follow-up note from Gladys:

> Dear Sir – Thank you very much for putting in your paper about the loss of my Mama Doll. I am sorry to say that I never got it back. But on Sunday morning a big car stopped at our home and a young lady Miss Olive Lake, of 67 Ormond Esplanade, Elwood, asked if Gladys Miller lived here and what do you think? She gave me a beautiful dressed doll, a big chocolate frog and another little toy. I am going to write and thank her for being so kind – Yours truly. GLADYS MILLER

I'm not crying. *You're* crying!

DOLL DRAMA 3

On 29 May 1933, an instance of stolen doll identification was reported in the Burnie *Advocate* under the heading 'Child Identifies Stolen Doll by Teeth-Marks':

> SYDNEY, Sunday – It is not often that a three-year-old child is called as a witness to identify stolen property, and her testimony accepted by the authorities. This occurred at Lithgow Police Station.

A large celluloid doll was found on the premises of the suspected person, and the child was able to identify it as hers by showing the police certain teeth-marks on the lips, toes and back of the head made by her infant sister.

I find this both endearing and disgusting. It's 'endgusting'.

DOLL DRAMA 4

On 13 September 1948, Sydney's *The Daily Telegraph* ran an article titled 'POLICE ASKED TO TRACE DOLL THIEF'. It describes the sad case of six-year-old Jeanette Bruce reporting her stolen doll to Marrickville Police. The young lady was out for revenge: 'She asked the sergeant in charge of Marrickville Police Station to get the biggest policeman he could "so that he can knock the thief's block off, and get my dolly back".'

Jeanette's mother told police her daughter was 'particularly fond' of the doll because 'it was dressed in kilts' (who doesn't love a splash of tartan?). The doll was taken from a stroller and a boy reported seeing 'another child wheeling the doll away'. The sergeant in charge 'said he had never before received a report of the theft of a doll'. Welcome to the big leagues, sergeant.

DOLL DRAMA 5

On 16 October 1950, a report titled 'Stolen Doll Recovered' was featured in the Adelaide tabloid *The News*. The article featured a photograph of Police Officer CE Lehmann holding an 'almost life size' doll with a retail value of £15 (equivalent to a whopping $900 in modern Aussie money). The extravagantly priced doll was stolen from a shop in Port Adelaide along with 'a cricket bat, two water pistols, boxing gloves, five combs, story books, five vases, and tennis balls'. Thankfully, the items were recovered, but the report fails to mention how. (*The News* wasn't known for its probing investigative journalism.)

DOLL DRAMA 6

On 7 April 1965, the *Windsor and Richmond Gazette* reported the case of 41-year-old Allan Sidney Walden stealing three ornamental dolls and a pot plant from a hotel in Windsor, NSW. The report was titled 'Stole Three Dolls: Three Months Gaol'. The dolls were valued at £15 each (that's a total value of A$1377) and belonged to Christine Podesta of Podesta's Hotel. The dolls were kept in a glass case in the hotel foyer and were stolen sometime between 3pm and 3.30pm on 28 January 1965. Salesperson Alan Walden (who was also a 'habitual criminal') was identified as one of the customers in the hotel at the time and confessed when questioned by police. 'Yes, it was a joke,' he told Detective Sergeant Shankleton. 'I sold the pot plant for a quid, but don't charge me. I'll get the dolls back to you.' Despite the confession, Walden pled not guilty and blamed 'a chap from the abattoirs'. The magistrate was unconvinced and sentenced Walden to three months in prison.

DOLL DRAMA 7

On 29 March 1972, *The Canberra Times* published a piece titled 'Raffle doll delayed'. The report began: 'In August 1970, Mrs G of Queanbeyan, won a "beautiful Italian dressed doll" as second prize in a raffle held by a sports club.' Unfortunately, the doll was stolen before it could be given to the winner. The raffle committee told Mrs G they would order a replacement from Italy, but after 19 months she was still without her prize. In a move worthy of *A Current Affair*, *The Canberra Times* contacted the president of the sports club to ask what the deal was with the missing doll. Turns out the substitution doll had arrived a couple of months earlier, but the people at the club had forgotten to give it to Mrs G. The club president 'was extremely apologetic about the delay and delivered the doll himself the next day at the home of Mrs G'. The article featured a photo of Mrs G with her doll, which was extravagantly dressed in 'Neapolitan costume'. You can tell from the photo that Mrs G was super stoked.

DOLL DRAMA 8

On 18 August 1993, an article titled 'Porcelain-doll heist leaves police stumped' ran in *The Canberra Times*. Tasmanian law enforcement was reportedly bemused by the theft of 50 porcelain dolls from a business in Launceston. The dolls belonged to Miriam Robinson, who proposed an interesting theory about the en masse doll disappearance. 'I suggested to the police that we go have a look in the park,' she said, 'because perhaps they'd gone out for a picnic or something, but they looked at me like I was a bit crazy.' (I can't imagine why.) The total collection was worth around $10,000. The police were 'stumped as to where the doll bandits might go to off-load their goods'. A month earlier, Tassie police had also been puzzled by the 'theft of 23 toilets as part of a plumbing supplies heist'. It looks like porcelain was hot property on the Tasmanian black market in 1993.

DOLL DRAMA 9

On 5 December 2017, *The Age* ran a piece titled 'Police hunt lonely adult shop thief who stole "Dorothy" the sex doll'. The masked robber used bolt cutters and a fire hydrant (this dude was determined!) to break into a Sexyland outlet in South Moorabbin, Melbourne at 6am on Sunday 3 December 2017. It looks like the thief had an eye on a very specific prize: 'a life-sized fantasy figurine with "ultra realistic feeling skin" and titanium alloy skeleton'. The doll was named 'Dorothy' (we're not in Kansas anymore, Toto). It carried a price tag of $4495. According to the report, the doll was 168cm tall, had blonde hair and was dressed in lingerie. The article featured a photo of Dorothy staring longingly into the distance.

DOLL DRAMA 10

On 8 February 2021, a similar robbery was reported by *Nine News* under the caption: 'Two men steal life-sized sex doll and other goods in raid at Sexyland store'. The thieves broke into the Airport West Sexyland at 2.45am on Tuesday 26 January 2021. They stole a $4500 sex doll named 'Kitty', along with 'multiple vibrators collectively worth about $10,000' (that sounds like quite the night in!). Kitty didn't survive the heist intact. Her head came unstuck in the car park and the thieves left it behind (rude). The duo drove off in a white Ford Ranger ute with their haul of vibrators and a decapitated sex doll. *Nine News* concluded with 'theft is common at adult entertainment stores and demand for dolls like Kitty and similar goods soared during the pandemic'. The report failed to mention anything about the demand for headless dolls, but I have no doubt there's a market for them as well.

In the words of Mark Twain: 'Man is the only animal that blushes – or needs to.' That pretty much says it all!

THE BAROSSA TEDDY BEAR
BEHEADINGS

ONCE I WAS DONE with doll-related crimes, the next logical step was to investigate teddy bear crimes. (How did this become my life?) I found several sad stories of plush bears stolen from small children. It was honestly heartbreaking. But there was one case that stood out. It was a cuddly toy crime that felt more like *Silence of the Lambs* than *Little Orphan Annie*.

In early 2018, the Barossa Valley town of Kapunda was rocked by the discovery of a teddy bear 'mass grave'. According to *The Advertiser*, five decapitated teddies were discovered on the outskirts of town, accompanied by this sinister note:

IF YOU GO DOWN TO THE
WOODS TODAY
YOU'RE SURE FOR A BIG SURPRISE
IF YOU GO DOWN TO THE
WOODS TODAY
YOU BETTER BE IN
DISGUISE!!!

That's some super disturbing 'rural noir' plush toy terror.

The unfortunate teddies belonged to a family of 15 bears. They were abducted from an advertising display set up by their owner, local mechanic Alex Boes. Alex told *The Advertiser* that the bears were 'beloved' by the community and were often seen hanging out at local landmarks. 'The bears are pretty famous,' he said, 'people come from all over the place to look for them in town.' So you can imagine the shock waves that rippled through the community when news of the massacre came to light.

But you can't keep a good teddy down. The beheaded bears were back in action a week later (with their heads securely reattached). They were proudly displayed on the second-storey balcony of the North Kapunda Hotel with a sign that read: 'You can't get us up here! Nah nah neh nan eh.' According to Alex, the teddies were 'quite happy' in their new spot and 'rather safe with a security camera'.

Alex also confirmed that the perpetrators had been found. The carnage was the work of a 'couple of kids' who got caught up in 'a moment of stupidity'. (I would have called it 'a moment of sociopathy'.) Alex generously opted to withhold the offenders' names so as not to 'embarrass them' (which is probably for the best, because their names would have been immortalised in this book). The kids received 'a good talking-to' before they 'all had a good laugh about it'.

I'm sure the bears weren't laughing.

BIZARRE LAW #7

Under Section 387 of the *Criminal Code Act 1913*, it is illegal to collect or remove seabird or bat poo (known as 'guano') 'from any part of the territorial dominions of WA without lawful authority'.

The unauthorised clean-up of guano in the state carries a maximum penalty of one year in prison. Imagine telling a gang of hardened criminals you were doing time because you cleaned bat poo off the bonnet of your car!

To be fair, guano was historically used to create gunpowder and explosives because of its rich nitrogen, phosphate and potassium content. But it's hard to understand why this law is still on the books. I doubt many Aussie criminals are scraping up shit to power their muskets like solders in the American Civil War.

BIZARRE LAW #8

The Trevi Fountain in Rome is famous for its coin-tossing traditions. It's said that if you toss a coin over your left-hand shoulder with your right hand, you will return to Rome; if you toss two coins, you'll find true love; and if you toss three coins, you'll be married in the eternal city. These traditions guarantee around $2.2 million worth of coins are thrown into the fountain every year (which is a total win for the Catholic charity Caritas, which gets to scoop up the proceeds).

Throwing coins into fountains dates back thousands of years. It's said to have begun with the ancient European practice of offering money to water spirits. The lucky-coin-in-a-fountain tradition is now observed all over the world. While nowhere is quite as busy or lucrative as the Trevi Fountain, it's rare to find a public fountain without at least a couple of coins lying at the bottom.

But beware NSW residents on the hunt for good fortune: you are technically breaking the law when you throw a coin in a fountain. Under Section 7 of the *Summary Offences Act 1988* (NSW), it is illegal to wilfully 'cause any foreign material or substance to enter into, any part of a fountain erected in a public place'. Coins qualify as a 'foreign material', which makes it an offence to toss 10 cents into the Archibald Memorial Fountain in Hyde Park. The maximum penalty is a $440 fine, which is quite the price to pay for making a wish!

In good news, it doesn't look like NSW cops are busy fining people for tossing coins into fountains. (I hope they have better things to do with their time.) In fact, the question of what to do with the many coins thrown into the fountains at Sydney's Parliament House became an issue of contention in 2005. At the time, the parliamentary services department collected around $200 per annum from the fountains at Sydney's Parliament House, which was deposited into the government's general revenue.

Labor senator John Faulkner told a senate estimates committee hearing he was surprised to learn the money wasn't given to charity. He told Department Secretary Hilary Penfold: 'I suspect some of the visitors who do this don't actually think that this money is going into your back pocket.' (I must be cynical because that's *exactly* where I thought the money would go.) After some initial pushback, Ms Penfold agreed to donate all the foreign coins collected to the Qantas and UNICEF 'Change for Good' program. With this in mind, I think the fine folk of NSW should ignore the law and toss coins into fountains with cheerful abandon! Even if their wish isn't granted, they may end up donating to a worthy cause.

(Disclaimer: the author assumes no responsibility or liability for any penalties the reader may incur from wistfully throwing a coin in a fountain. If the reader receives a fine from a mean-spirited law enforcement officer who is over-compensating for an inferiority complex they developed as a child, that's officially not my problem.)

SOMETHING OFF IN THE PANTRY

'FOR A PERSON LIVING with brain cancer ... you look incredibly healthy,' said *Sunrise* host Samantha Armytage. The year was 2014 and the person looking 'incredibly healthy' was twenty-something Belle Gibson, who *was* looking remarkably well for someone diagnosed with terminal cancer. In fact, Belle didn't just look 'healthy' – she looked positively radiant. (To this day, I would love to know her skincare regimen.)

The young wellness influencer first caught the public's eye in early 2013 with the launch of her Instagram account @healing_belle. The page documented Belle's miraculous journey to health after she received a shocking cancer diagnosis in 2009. Doctors told her she had a 'malignant brain tumour' and gave her a maximum of four months to live. According to Belle, she spent two months undergoing chemotherapy and radiation treatment before deciding to take an alternative approach. She embarked on a 'quest' to heal herself through 'nutrition, patience, determination and love'. Belle employed a host of natural therapies, including colonics, craniosacral therapy, oxygen therapy and Ayurvedic treatments. She also adopted a 'whole food', plant-based diet, free from dairy, gluten, GMOs, preservatives and sugar (sounds like fun). Much of her Instagram page was dedicated to sharing her favourite cancer-defying recipes.

Belle's story and recipes soon gained an online following of over 200,000. Belle launched 'The Whole Pantry' mobile app in August 2013, which *The Herald Sun* described as 'the world's first health, wellness and lifestyle app ... [encouraging] healthy eating, positive thinking and a wholesome lifestyle'. The app was downloaded 200,000 times within the first month and named 'Apple's Best Food and Drink App of 2013'. She also signed a book deal with Lantern Books (a subsidiary of Penguin) for a 'Whole Pantry' cookbook. She was working with a team of eight to share her message of natural medicine and wellness. Things were going gangbusters.

Then, in July 2014, Belle took to social media to share some bad news: 'I have cancer in my blood, spleen, brain, uterus and liver. I am hurting ... I wanted to respectfully let you each know, and hand some of the energy over to the greater community, my team and @thewhole-pantry ... Please don't carry my pain. I've got this.' The outpouring of love and support was huge. Everyone was rooting for Belle.

But the love and support dried up when it was revealed in early 2015 that Belle's cancer claims were completely fabricated. In an interview with *The Australian Women's Weekly* in April 2015, Belle confessed that 'none of it [was] true' and she didn't 'really understand how cancer works'.

Belle had also been less than truthful about her childhood, name, age and general medical history. Her devoted followers were understandably outraged. There was a special fury reserved for those innocent 'Whole Pantry' devotees battling cancer who had eschewed conventional treatments to follow Belle's 'all-natural' approach.

'I don't want forgiveness,' Belle told *The Women's Weekly*. 'I just think [speaking out] was the responsible thing to do. Above anything, I would like people to say, "Okay, she's human. She's obviously had a big life. She's respectfully come to the table and said what she's needed to say, and now it's time for her to grow and heal".'

'The Whole Pantry' brand was defunct. Apple pulled the app and Penguin pulled the book. Belle's wellness empire was in tatters. In hopes of 'clearing the air', she agreed to an interview with Tara Brown on *60 Minutes*. It was a PR move worthy of Prince Andrew.

(I have a confession: my main reason for telling this story was to quote the Tara Brown interview. It's one of the most unhinged interviews in human history. If NASA ever sends another Voyager probe to deep space, I pray they pack a recording of this conversation for alien civilisations to decode.)

In mid-2015, Belle sat across from Tara in a heavy-knit pink turtleneck sweater that made me feel hot just looking at it. If the turtleneck wasn't enough to make Belle sweat, Tara's withering remarks must have done the trick:

Tara: You go on Instagram in 2013: 'I have been healing severe and malignant brain cancer for the past few years, with natural medicine, Gerson therapy and foods. It's working for me'.
Belle: It is.
Tara: Except you didn't have brain cancer.
Belle: No, I didn't. But when I was writing that I thought that I did. And I was feeling well.
Tara: Yes, but even then, you misrepresented what you thought was your truth, which was all a big lie, anyway.

Belle explained that she never received a formal cancer diagnosis from a credentialed medical professional. Rather, she was told she had a stage 4 brain tumour by a shadowy 'integrative medicine' practitioner named Dr Mark Johns, who diagnosed Belle at her home using 'a machine with lights on the front'. (Dr Mark Johns was unavailable for comment because there's no record of him existing.)

The interview continued:

Tara: Why did you write in the foreword of your book that you got this information in your doctor's office ...?

Belle: Because I think that being open and telling people the way that it happened would, um, not be understood and that people would be disappointed and angry for me not, um, following what is the right way to go about this.

Tara: So you lied because you feared you wouldn't be believed, is that what you're saying?

Belle: Um, it's not what I'm saying.

Tara: Well, can you be clearer in what you're saying? I mean, you were absolutely misleading, weren't you? You said a doctor gave you this terrible prognosis in his office and you've just admitted that you didn't say it was at your home and it wasn't with a real doctor because you thought people would be disappointed in you.

Belle: I believed he was a real doctor.

Tara: So, did you lie to be believed, is the question?

Belle: I didn't see him in his doctor's office in Perth.

Tara: You didn't see him in his doctor's office ever, because he doesn't have an office, does he?

Belle: No.

Tara questioned Belle about the myriad medical conditions and operations she described on an online skateboarding forum in 2009:

Tara: 2009 was a really bad year for you, wasn't it? You had three heart operations, you suffered two cardiac arrests, you died twice on the operating table, you had a stroke and you were diagnosed with an inoperable brain tumour and given four months to live.

Belle: Correct.

Of course, none of this was 'correct' because it was all lies. To her credit,

Belle conceded that she *didn't* have three heart surgeries or die twice on the operating table, which was a step in the right direction. But Tara wasn't about to let her off the hook, especially when Belle tried to excuse her fabrications as the actions of a 'melodramatic' teenager:

> **Tara:** Melodramatic? They're straight out lies. You weren't in hospital – you were claiming you were. You claimed you died twice. You didn't. You claimed you had two cardiac arrests. You didn't. That's not melodramatic. That's straight out lying.
>
> **Belle:** It is.
>
> **Tara:** Extraordinary lies.

Belle knew she was cancer-free long before she told the truth to the public. Tara brought receipts, including a neurologist's report from 2011, clearly stating that Belle *didn't* have a brain tumour. (Strangely enough, it was Belle who provided the damning medical documents to *60 Minutes* producers.)

Belle continued to answer Tara's questions with lies. These lies conflicted with other lies, thereby creating an elaborate matrix of lies that's too complex for any reasonable human being to unpack:

> **Tara:** Do you know what the definition of truth is?
>
> **Belle:** Yes.
>
> **Tara:** What's your definition of truth?
>
> **Belle:** Um, speaking with honesty and, um, with clear definition around fact.
>
> **Tara:** And what's your definition of a lie?
>
> **Belle:** Obviously, the opposite of that.
>
> **Tara** [reading from her notes]: 'A false statement made with deliberate intention to deceive, an intentional untruth, a falsehood.'
>
> **Belle:** And I've not been intentionally untruthful. I've been openly

conveying and speaking about what was my reality, and what is my reality today.

Tara: Do you accept that your reality does not actually match reality?

Belle: It doesn't match your normal or your reality ...

But the crowning moment was when Tara asked Belle to clarify her age, which proved far more challenging than anyone might have imagined:

Tara: You're 23, right? Well, actually, how old are you?

Belle: Um, I've always been raised, um, as being currently a 26-year-old.

Tara: How old are you?

Belle: Well, I live knowing, as I've always known, I would be 26.

Tara: Okay, Belle. This is a really, really simple question. How old are you?

Belle: I believe that I'm 26. I have two birth certificates and I've had my name changed four times. The identity crisis there is big. But that was my normal growing up, Tara ...

Tara: What do you know the truth to be now?

Belle: It's probably a question we'll have to keep digging for, because it's not something I've ever understood or had answers around.

Tara's no-holds-barred interview style was universally applauded. People loved watching her throw shade at the fraudster like a drag queen heckling their audience at 3am. Belle finished the interview looking very sad indeed. And things were about to get worse.

Lying about cancer is heinous and immoral, but it's not a 'crime'. What *is* a crime is to use your non-existent cancer diagnosis to defraud consumers (which Belle did). It is also a crime to claim that you're going to donate money raised through fundraisers and the sales of your app and then fail to make those donations (which also happened, to the tune of $300,000).

In September 2017, Belle was ordered to pay $410,000 in fines for contraventions of Australian consumer law. Belle didn't show up to the court proceedings and made no effort to explain (or apologise for) her actions. Justice Debbie Mortimer was less than impressed: 'In looking at the total sum which is appropriate to make Ms Gibson pay, there can be no allowance made for contrition, remorse, apology or acceptance of responsibility by Ms Gibson,' said Justice Mortimer. 'Once again, it appears she has put her own interests before those of anyone else ... If there is one theme or pattern which emerges through her conduct, it is her relentless obsession with herself and what best serves her interests.'

Whack!

In 2019, Belle was summoned back to court after she failed to pay any of her fines. Belle claimed she was unable to pay the fines because she was broke. However, her financial records told a different story.

'[The documents] reveal a great many transactions overwhelmingly in the nature of discretionary spending,' said Consumer Affairs Victoria barrister Elle Nikou Madalin. These transactions included payments for cryptocurrency, futures trading and sports betting. *A Current Affair* also busted Belle returning from a five-week luxury safari in East Africa. It was revealed that Belle had spent $91,000 between 2017 and 2019. The court once again ordered Belle to pay her fines.

In 2020, Belle claimed to be a member of Ethiopia's Oromo community in Melbourne. Dressed in an Ethiopian headscarf, the exotic-looking Belle told an interviewer her name was 'Sabontu' and she had been volunteering with the Oromo community for the past four years. 'My heart is deeply embedded in the Oromo people,' she said. 'I feel blessed to be adopted by you.'

The president of the Australian Oromo Community Association in Victoria, Dr Tarekegn Chimdi, was quick to refute Belle's claims. She was *never* a registered volunteer and he'd only seen her at community events 'two or three times'. 'She is not a community member and she's also not working with the community,' said Chimdi. 'She has to stop [telling people she is].' As far as I can tell, Belle stopped using the 'Sabontu' alias after that.

In 2021, the Victorian Sheriff's officer executed a 'seizure and sale' warrant at Belle's home in the hopes of recouping some of the unpaid fines. When *A Current Affair* confronted her in early 2024, she had yet to pay a single cent. Belle was upset by the interviewer's line of questioning and asked him to 'show some humanity', which is a tad ironic. She claimed to be broke and unable to find employment, but she still looked incredibly healthy.

BIZARRE LAW #9

For most of us, kite-flying evokes thoughts of childhood, sunshine and faraway dreams. It's hard to imagine anyone hating kites. It's like hating the joy of wonder.

But not everyone's a fan. Under Section 4 of the *Summary Offences Act 1966* (Vic), it's an offence for Victorians to fly a kite 'to the annoyance of any person'. The legislation lists this offence with several other offences 'relating to the good order towns etc', including burning 'rubbish shavings or other materials' in a public place, leaving 'inflammable materials' in a public place, setting off fireworks without permission and opening 'a drain or sewer' without authorisation. I'm sure you'll agree that flying a kite seems slightly less serious than burning trash in public or randomly setting off fireworks. But not in Victoria! If you're found guilty of 'annoying' kite flying, you can face a maximum fine of $961.55.

A warning to Victorians: next time a cheerful chimney sweep invites you to 'go fly a kite', make sure you survey the area for any disgruntled onlookers before you launch your fragile craft upon the wind. You don't want your charming day out to go from *Mary Poppins* to an episode of *Highway Patrol*.

A NOT-SO-ROYAL AFFAIR

JOEL [REDACTED] WAS THE 'party prince' of late noughties Brisbane. He was a regular at the fabulous Cloudland nightclub, sipping top-shelf champagne and showering waitstaff with four-figure tips. He dressed in designer clothes, wore a Chanel watch, drove Mercedes-Benz sports cars and owned a $5 million waterfront home. His collection of luxury goods included a life-sized 'horse lamp', a Hermès saddle and a Louis Vuitton surfboard. (I wonder what the surfer bros thought when Joel rocked up to the beach carrying his branded board.)

Joel claimed his extravagant lifestyle was courtesy of his family, who happened to be the Tahitian Royal Family. According to Joel, he was a member of the ruling dynasty of the Kingdom of Tahiti tracing back to King Pōmare I. If anyone wanted evidence, he could flash his black American Express card, which bore the initials 'HRH' (standing for 'His Royal Highness') in front of his name. Unfortunately, Joel was forced to hold a job to access his inheritance. This was why he spent his days as a middle manager for Queensland Health (it's important to instil exotic princes with a solid work ethic).

In case you hadn't guessed, Joel's story was a lie. He was not a Tahitian prince. He was a New Zealander. He did not have an elaborate allowance. He got his money by defrauding massive sums from Queensland Health.

Joel siphoned almost $17 million from his employer via 62 fraudulent transactions made between 2007 and 2011. He set up a fake charity called 'Filling the Gap' to pretend the payments were part of a government grant scheme (as if stealing millions from a health body isn't bad enough!). Police were finally alerted when Joel made a transfer of $11 million in December 2011.

Police raided his apartment on 12 December 2011. They found Joel unconscious in bed (he'd been enjoying some of the party drugs the police found at his home). He was arrested and charged with fraud and drug possession. Police confiscated everything, including the surfboard.

Joel pled guilty to all charges. At his sentencing in 2013, Judge Kerry O'Brien described his spending as 'extreme'. Judge O'Brien said the multi-year fraud was an 'audacious scheme' to 'obtain an opulent and extravagant lifestyle' (the judge was going hard on adjectives that day).

Joel's defence barrister said his client's crime 'was a simple fraud which was bound to be discovered'. The party prince had been waiting for the other shoe to drop (in this case, a black patent leather Christian Louboutin with a red sole and tone-on-tone grosgrain piping finish).

Joel was sentenced to 14 years in prison, with a non-parole period of five. Upon his release from Wolston Correctional Centre in 2020, he received a not-so-royal escort to the airport. Australian Border Force officers put him on a flight to New Zealand, where he went to live with his mother.

I'm guessing he flew economy.

ID-IOTIC

CATCHING A CROOK CAN be hard work. Police must often rely on incomplete evidence, hostile witnesses and unreliable testimony. Drawing together the fragments of a case can be like building a jigsaw puzzle with half the pieces missing.

Catching a crook can also be remarkably easy, especially when criminals leave behind their personal information and/or contact details at a crime scene. Here are three examples of foolish felons who have done exactly that.

IDIOTIC INCIDENT 1

On 8 April 2019, 19-year-old Kian [Redacted] was caught trying to steal a car from a home in Edmonton, Cairns. He fled the scene but left behind a remarkably revealing backpack of evidence. *The Cairns Post* reported that the bag contained Kian's 'birth certificate, tax documents, a court charge sheet for another matter and a mobile phone featuring multiple selfies'. (It's always nice when criminals provide the cops with 50 points of ID.)

Kian appeared at Cairns Magistrates Court a couple of days later, where prosecutor Natalie Keys described his actions as 'extremely brazen ... and incredibly stupid'. I don't think anyone was surprised when he pleaded guilty. If you leave your birth certificate at the scene of the crime, that's pretty much your only option.

IDIOTIC INCIDENT 2

On 22 October 2020, Canberra radio presenter Annabelle Brett woke up to a phone notification that her car alarm had been triggered. A friend checked Annabelle's parking garage and confirmed the vehicle was missing. Annabelle's $70,000 Model 3 Tesla had been stolen.

Annabelle caught a ride with her friend and used the Tesla's tracking app to chase the stolen vehicle. While in hot pursuit, she used the Tesla app to limit the car's speed limit, honk the horn and roll the windows up and down. The thieves must have known they were in trouble because they pulled into a public park a couple of blocks from Annabelle's house. She arrived in time to see a man in a high-vis shirt get out of her Tesla and switch into a blue Ford Fiesta driven by another man.

'I started filming as I approached the scene where they'd pulled over,' she told *The Daily Mail*. 'They left my car and started driving off and flipped me the bird.' (Rude.)

When Annabelle inspected her car, she discovered the thief had dropped a driver's licence in an addressed envelope. This led police straight to the perpetrators, who were on outstanding warrants. The main culprit was charged with joint commission minor theft, joint commission taking a motor vehicle without consent, failure to appear after bail undertaking, and first instance warrant. Annabelle hoped her story would deter potential car thieves. 'There's just so much technology now,' she said, 'you're bound to be caught.' (You're also bound to be caught if you leave a driver's licence in the car you stole.)

IDIOTIC INCIDENT 3

On 8 August 2022, 34-year-old Aaron [Redacted] was found guilty by Judge Timothy Heffernan at Adelaide District Court of illegally possessing a firearm. Aaron became a wanted man in March 2020 after he cut off his detention bracelet and escaped house arrest. Police tracked him down to a home in Elizabeth Vale. The cops searched a Holden sedan parked outside and recovered a Nike bum bag containing Aaron's wallet, bank cards and ID. It also contained socks, underwear, a camouflage balaclava, eight cartridges of ammunition and a fully loaded sawn-off Winchester single-barrel 12-gauge shotgun.

Aaron's lawyer took a strangely insulting approach to defending his client. He began by admitting that Aaron was 'not the sharpest tool in the shed'. Nevertheless, he doubted his client would be foolish enough to leave such incriminating evidence in his bum bag. 'He's not a person who is not worldly wise ... in the sense of being involved in criminal activity,' said Aaron's lawyer. 'He's not going to be a person who puts on gloves, grabs a hold of eight cartridges, puts them into his own bag, leaves them in his own bag when he's on the run from the police, knowing full well they are looking for him.'

Judge Heffernan disagreed. He thought Aaron was exactly the kind of person to store an illegal firearm and ammunition in a Nike bum bag with his ID, underpants and a camouflage balaclava while on the run from the police. 'By his own admission,' said the judge, 'his bum bag was an essential item which he took with him everywhere.' On top of the sentence he was already serving, Aaron was sentenced to eight years and one month in prison. He really should have stayed at home.

I can't help feeling sorry for Aaron. I'm 100 per cent sure he was guilty, but it still sucks when your signature fashion accessory becomes the deciding evidence in your trial for possession of a sawn-off shotgun after your lawyer has used the 'my client is stupid, but not *that* stupid' defence. That's what I call a bad day in court.

THE PRIME MINISTER'S DOOR HANDLE

THE 2003 RUGBY WORLD Cup final was a tough loss for Australia. The close match against England saw the Aussies fall short of victory by only three points. Wallabies lock forward Justin Harrison was gutted by the defeat and threw his silver medal into Darling Harbour. It was a decision he would come to regret.

Prime Minister John Howard invited the defeated team to the Lodge for a cheer-up dinner. The boys were eager to let off some steam and happy to make use of the PM's bar facilities. In true larrikin style, several teammates resolved to pocket pieces of memorabilia. Harrison chose an antique doorhandle – embossed with a coat of arms – positioned on a toilet door. He excused himself throughout the evening to 'use the facilities' and loosened the handle with a knife.

Harrison explained the caper on Stan Sport's *Rugby Heaven* in 2021. 'By the end of the night I had it – in my pocket, out the door,' he said. 'I was pretty proud of myself on the bus, showing everyone that I'd got this.' Other teammates had only managed small-time stuff such as salt shakers and teaspoons. Harrison was the night's gold medal thief. (I'm not sure what Harrison was planning on doing with the doorhandle. Perhaps he was going to secure it to the door of his own toilet for that classic 'pooping prime minister' feel.)

A couple of days later, Harrison received an unexpected call. The caller introduced himself as Constable Thompson from the Australian Federal Police (AFP). He told Harrison that the AFP had been reviewing CCTV footage from the Wallabies' visit to the Lodge. They were trying to locate a missing door handle.

'It's a heritage-listed property,' said Constable Thompson. '[It's] the Prime Minister's property and it's a crime against the Commonwealth and in fact the Queen.'

Uh-oh. Harrison assured Constable Thompson he would call around his teammates to help locate the stolen item. He asked how the doorhandle might be returned without any further police involvement. Constable Thompson said the best option would be to simply post the doorhandle back to the Lodge.

Harrison hung up and headed straight to the post office. He sent the doorhandle priority post to the Lodge, listing the sender as 'John Smith'. Job done.

Twenty-five minutes later Harrison received a call from the Wallabies physician Martin Raftery. The good doctor couldn't help laughing as he informed Harrison that 'Constable Thompson' was, in fact, Raftery's son. There was no AFP investigation. The prankster had been pranked.

'Not only have I been tricked, I've lost my memorabilia,' said Harrison. 'I've lost my handle because it's in a priority paid package in parcel post on its way to ... the Lodge.'

But perhaps Harrison earned some good karma when he returned the stolen property. In July 2022, Rugby Football Union president Jeff Blackett gave Harrison a replacement World Cup silver medal. An emotional Harrison couldn't help shedding a few tears of joy. He was finally able to show his sons the medal their dad won at the 2003 World Cup.

They say 'what goes around, comes around'. It's nice to know Harrison's silver medal found its way home. Hopefully the doorhandle did as well.

EGGED ON

I F YOU VISIT THE town of Warwick in the Darling Downs region of southeast Queensland, I recommend popping to the train station and checking out the information sign that stands out front. The sign bears the title: 'Billy Hughes and Formation of the Federal Police.' It briefly tells the story of the so-called 'Warwick Egg Incident' ('WEGGI' for short) and the impact it had on the history of Australian law enforcement:

> On 29th November, 1917, on the platform of the Warwick Railway Station, the Prime Minister of Australia W. M. (Billy) Hughes, who was returning to the south, attempted to address the assembled towns-people in support of the controversial issue of conscription.
>
> The crowd was restive and a well aimed egg soon removed Billy Hughes' hat. He immediately demanded the arrest of the culprit for a breach of the Commonwealth Law.
>
> Snr. Sgt. Kenny of the Warwick Police and upholder of the Queensland Law only, refused to take any action and Hughes departed vowing vengeance.
>
> From this small incident at a turbulent time towards the close of World War I was born the Federal Police Force.

Who would have guessed a couple of 'well aimed' eggs would be worthy of a public sign? But the story made national headlines and obviously caused Billy Hughes some serious emotional distress.

The Prime Minister had been on the campaign trail, fighting a bitter battle to institute compulsory national conscription. He held a referendum on the issue in October 1916, which failed to get over the line. Hughes was committed to the cause and determined to hold another referendum in December 1917. Queensland Premier TJ Ryan was a vocal opponent of conscription, so Hughes decided to take a tour of the Sunshine State to drum up grassroots support.

On that fateful day in November 1917, the Prime Minister arrived in Warwick by train, where he was greeted by local officials. He walked across the platform to greet a crowd of residents and give a speech on the importance of conscription.

That's when the eggs began to fly.

The first egg was launched from the crowd, missing the Prime Minister and splashing the dresses of some nearby ladies. The second egg knocked Hughes's hat clean off his head. An article published in the *Warwick Argus* two days later described the ensuing commotion:

[I]n an instant all was tumult, excitement and confusion ... It was very difficult from the first to follow the various phases of the disturbances, as so many things were happening all at once, and the crowd was surging back and forward over the platform in a condition of intense excitement, caused mainly by the unexpected fistic encounters.

Don't you hate it when 'unexpected fistic encounters' break out at your pro-national service rural train station rally?

The culprits responsible for the errant eggs were Bart and Patrick Brosnan, two brothers of Irish descent who were *not* supportive of compulsory conscription. As the *Warwick Argus* tells it, a member of the crowd launched at Patrick in response to the egg-throwing. Bart leapt to his brother's defence and things got physical:

> [T]hen there was a wild scrimmage, in which arms and fists could be seen working vigorously. Bart Brosnan, towering above the crowd, had blood on his face, and the scene at this stage of the proceedings threatened to develop seriously ... Everybody seemed to be rushing towards the combatants, but fortunately, the fighting ended almost as quickly as it began.

Don't you hate it when you get blood on your face in a 'wild scrimmage' after your brother throws an egg at the Prime Minister at a pro-national service rural train station rally?

Once the spectacle died down, Hughes was spotted in an 'animated discussion' with Senior Sergeant Kenny of the Queensland Police. The Prime Minister was upset by the officer's refusal to arrest the Brosnan brothers. According to Kenny, he couldn't arrest the brothers because they hadn't broken any state laws. (I was going to investigate the Queensland legislation of the era regarding egg-throwing, but I couldn't be bothered. We'll just have to take Kenny's word for it.) Hughes argued that Commonwealth law trumped state law and the Brosnans should be arrested regardless. Kenny stood his ground and the brothers remained free. An outraged Prime Minister sent a strongly worded telegram to the Queensland Commissioner for Police later that day:

> At Warwick today at 3 pm when leaving the train to address a public meeting I was assaulted by a number of men STOP there was great tumult amounting virtually to a riot STOP I ordered the police to immediately arrest the two most prominent ring leaders but acting under the Senior Sergt's direction they refused to do so STOP

He continued to say that Kenny 'connived at the disgraceful proceedings' and was also in breach of Commonwealth law. Hughes insisted the Senior Sargeant be suspended immediately. If the Queensland Police Commissioner failed to comply, the Commonwealth Government would be forced to 'take steps to enforce its own laws'.

The telegram didn't once mention the word 'egg'.

If you're getting 'drama queen' energy from the Prime Minister's telegram, you're not alone. In fact, Brisbane's *Daily Standard* published an article a few days later titled: 'Warwick Affair – Lies Blown Out – What Really Happened – Hughes Not Assaulted – His Hysterics Due to One Egg.' The article did *not* hold back on taking the Prime Minister to task:

> On the day after the event, 'The Daily Standard' was able to publish first hand accounts by eye-witnesses ... It was shown that Mr. Hughes was not assaulted – beyond the rotten egg hitting his hat; that he was NOT called upon to fight a mob of anarchists single-handed; and that instead of coming out of the episode the hero that his publicity agents claimed him to be, he came out with very bad grace as a political bounder who attempted to act the dictator over Queensland police-men, and who, in a disgraceful fury, viciously libelled the crowd of people who had come to greet him.
>
> The paper has no time for rotten eggs. It objects to them being thrown at anybody ... A Prime Minister suffering the indignity of having his hat hit with a stale egg has our sympathy, but he sends – or allows to be sent – a misleading report calculated to give the public the impression that the egg-thrower was a bomb thrower, and the police are traitors, he deserves no sympathy. On the contrary, he is worthy of public condemnation.

But shady editorials weren't enough to stop Hughes's pursuit of justice. Shortly after the incident, he drafted legislation to create the

Commonwealth Police Force (CPF) so no Australian would again have to suffer the indignity of an unprosecuted egg assault. (There were also other, less ridiculous reasons for establishing the CPF, but I won't go into them because they're not as entertaining.) The CPF only lasted two years, but it laid the foundation for future federal law enforcement, culminating in the creation of the AFP in 1979. All because of two Irish egg-throwers and a highly sensitive Prime Minister.

A hundred and two years later, another politically motivated egg incident made national headlines when a schoolboy cracked an egg on the head of far-right Queensland senator Fraser Anning.

On 15 March 2019, Anning tweeted comments about Muslims, immigration and the Christchurch massacre. I'm not going to repeat Anning's comments because they're not worth repeating, but his remarks were condemned from all sides of politics as 'disgusting', 'appalling', 'ugly', 'horrific', 'racist' and 'contemptible'.

Anning gave a press conference in Melbourne the following day. A young man in a white T-shirt was standing with the crowd of journalists surrounding the senator. The fresh-faced lad was holding up a phone and appeared to be a member of the media. In one swift move, the young man used his free arm to smash an egg into the senator's head. Anning spun around and smacked his 'egg-ressor' in the face. There was a brief exchange of blows before they were forced apart by onlookers and the young man was tackled to the ground.

The 17-year-old was dubbed 'Egg Boy' on social media and a video of the encounter went viral online. He was lauded as a national hero and a GoFundMe campaign was set up to cover his legal fees (and the cost of 'more eggs'). Egg Boy got away with a warning, so he donated the $100,000 raised to victims of the Christchurch massacre. As for Anning, he was censured by parliament, lost his senate seat at the 2019 election, went bankrupt and fled to the US.

In an interview with *The Daily Mail* in 2021, Egg Boy suggested there might be another egg scramble in the making. 'I've been saying that I have one egg left for someone special,' he said. 'I just don't know who it is yet.'

Hopefully he's true to his word. Australians don't want to wait another 102 years for their next national egg incident!

EMERGENCY DISSERVICES

IMPERSONATING A POLICE OFFICER can land you in prison for up to two years, or it can turn you into a laughing-stock on social media. It all depends.

On November 2016, a woman was reported driving a 'fake police car' in Perth's CBD. According to *The Guardian,* the 33-year-old was operating a dented white Hyundai with the word 'POLICE' drawn on the side in blue felt pen. She had also drawn on police-style blue-and -white chequers, just to ramp up the authenticity level. It's fair to say the woman's handiwork resembled what a nine-year-old might craft for a school project.

Police pulled her over and the vehicle was seized. She wasn't charged with impersonating a police officer, because the drawing couldn't really be considered an 'impersonation'. (In fact, the drawing didn't break any laws at all, although it did break several rules of good taste.) She *was* charged with driving an unroadworthy vehicle without a driver's license and given notice to appear in court at a later date. Meanwhile, images of the Hyundai created much hilarity as they made the rounds on Facebook.

A year later, a 16-year-old Melbourne boy was also making headlines for driving a fake emergency vehicle. But unlike his Perth counterpart, the teenager had done a much better job of impersonating the genuine article. His white Isuzu truck was decked out with flashing red-and-blue lights, sirens and a rear spotlight. It was estimated the modifications had set him back over $100,000.

The young man spent weeks careering through St Kilda and Elwood, sirens blaring and cars making way. He responded several times to real-life emergencies and even offered help to people in accidents. (I'm not sure I'd feel terribly comforted seeing a 16-year-old paramedic running towards me in an emergency.) But his luck ran out on 17 October 2017 when detectives from the Heavy Vehicle Crime Investigation Unit saw online footage of him driving along Beach Road in St Kilda. He was arrested in the wealthy suburb of Brighton, which may explain how a 16-year-old could afford a six-figure truck upgrade. *Nine News* reported that when the teenager was arrested, he said: 'I think I've been doing something stupid.' Ya think?

Another imitation emergency vehicle was spotted in Melbourne in 2023. This time, witnesses reported seeing a fake Chinese police car making its way around town. People were surprised to spot a black Nissan sedan bearing the Chinese characters for 'police' and 'ministry of public security' roaming the streets of West Melbourne. Some raised concerns the Chinese Communist Party was responsible. Others suggested it was an over-eager fan of Chinese law enforcement. Either way, the Victorian Police didn't seem to mind. A spokesperson told media outlets that 'no specific offences' had been committed and the police had 'not received any reports in relation to the matter'.

I have to say, the laws regarding emergency-vehicle-inspired car decoration seem rather relaxed. If it's okay to rock an imitation Chinese police car, what else can you get away with? Is it cool to deck out your family's Toyota RAV4 in the orange insignia of an Italian ambulance, with 'AMBULANZA' emblazoned backwards on the bonnet? How about sporting the two-headed yellow eagle crest of the Albanian 'POLICIA' on the driver's front door of your Ford Ranger? If Dubai police get to roll around in green-and-white Lamborghini Aventadors, why can't you? After all, nothing says 'well-endowed man with a good sense of self' like a dude driving a Chevrolet Corvette Z06 fitted out with a scaled-down imitation Bosnian fire engine ladder.

BRUSH WITH THE LAW

HAIR HAS HELD SPECIAL significance in cultures throughout history and around the world. Ancient Egyptian pharaohs wore elaborate wigs as a show of status. Young Native American warriors styled their hair into mohawks as a sign of bravery. To this day, hair is still widely recognised as a symbol of vitality, strength, wealth and youth. In the modern beauty business, hair is a prized commodity that drives a multi-million-dollar industry. For others, it holds an erotic allure (try googling 'trichophilia'). Hair is something people want. It's also something people steal.

In March 2007, Sydney Airport baggage handler Rodney [Redacted] faced court on charges of stealing women's hair from their luggage. The 30-year-old acquired the hair by rifling through lost and delayed bags before returning them to passengers. He removed the hair from brushes and clothing, inserted it into plastic slips and catalogued information about the hair's 'owners' in an exercise book. Police found over 80 bags of hair in Rodney's 'collection'. His lawyer claimed his client wasn't trying to scare anyone because his victims weren't supposed to find out. Based on previous convictions, Rodney was sentenced to a maximum of two years and eight months in jail.

Another creepy hair theft was reported in Melbourne in December 2015. A man accosted a woman walking in the CBD early in the morning.

The unnamed assailant grabbed the woman's hair and chopped a piece off with a pair of scissors before running off. The woman screamed (as you would) and a couple of bystanders ran to her aid. To help with their investigations, police released a facial composite portrait of the hair mugger. (He looked like a low-rent fire twirler with a side hustle participating in clinical trials for experimental medicines.) There were no follow-up reports, so we can only assume he's living his best life scouring the dumpsters behind his local beauty parlour.

Of course, not all hair crimes are weird, fetish-related offences. A rather high-class, historical hair heist was committed in 2014 when a lock of Napoleon Bonaparte's hair was stolen from the Briars in Mount Martha, Victoria. Burglars broke into the homestead after 11pm on 10 April, jemmied open cabinets and took several 'priceless' artefacts belonging to the French military leader. Ten items were stolen, including the lock of hair, a miniature portrait, a ribbon, a ring, a silver inkwell and a snuff box. Police suggested the items may have been taken on behalf of a wealthy private collector (immediately evoking images of a Bond villain living in a volcano surrounded by early 19th-century military memorabilia). The thieves were not found, and the trail went cold until 2022 when a Sydney art dealer bought a miniature portrait of Joséphine Bonaparte on eBay for $250. He realised his purchase was one of the stolen items and immediately contacted the Briars. Police couldn't confirm or deny the status of the other artefacts. As far as we know, Napoleon's hair is still out there.

Then there was the big hair robbery of 2018. Over $100,000 worth of hair extensions were stolen from a salon in the Melbourne suburb of Craigieburn. In the early hours of Saturday 1 December, thieves reversed a ute through the salon's front doors and burst into the shop. As one *Seven News* reporter said: 'It's an unusual setting for a brush with the law.' (Get it? Brush?)

Two masked men leapt from the vehicle while another waited in the driver's seat. In a matter of minutes, the burglars made off with hundreds of packets of authentic human hair (in a variety of lengths and colours, including dark browns, blondes and two-tone mixes). The ute was later discovered dumped in Greenvale, but the thieves were nowhere to be found. The extensions were valued at up to $250 a packet (the same price as a stolen Napoleonic miniature on eBay) and it was expected the hair would be sold online at a discounted rate. For the owners of the salon, losing all that stock in the lead-up to Christmas was a very bad hair day indeed.

METH BUSTERS

IT'S HARDLY SURPRISING WHEN a meth dealer does something self-destructive – it goes with the territory. But the following stories of meth dealers making poor life decisions give new meaning to 'being your own worst enemy'.

Twenty-three-year-old Jake [Redacted] appeared before Rockhampton Supreme Court in September 2017 on drugs and weapons charges. He landed himself in the dock after driving to the Rockhampton Police Complex to report for bail. He was disqualified from driving at the time (mistake #1), so he hid the keys to his car in a nearby garden. An onlooker saw this, retrieved the keys, took them into the station and told police they belonged to Jake. Police searched Jake's car and discovered he had driven to the station carrying a handgun (mistake #2), a self-loading firearm (mistake #3), two vials of steroids (mistake #4), seven brass knuckle dusters (mistake #5) and 19.917 grams of crystal meth (mistake #6). In passing sentence, Justice Duncan McMeekin said the circumstances of the arrest were 'almost comical'. (I'd drop the 'almost'.)

Jake was disqualified from driving for two years, disqualified from holding a firearms licence and sentenced to two years in prison. The *New Zealand Herald* reported this case with the headline: 'Is Queenslander

Jake [Redacted] Australia's dumbest criminal?' And maybe he was, at least until the next story came along.

Twenty-eight-year-old Simon [Redacted] appeared before the NSW District Court in September 2020 on drug trafficking charges. On the morning of 22 July 2019, Simon was driving his Toyota HiAce through north-west Sydney when he dozed off. His van drifted across the road and crashed into two police vehicles parked at Eastwood Police Station. He left the scene of the accident without leaving his contact details (rude) and police went in search of the driver. They tracked him down an hour later and asked him some questions. Simon was visibly nervous and avoided eye contact with the officers. He claimed he was delivering food and had fallen into a 'microsleep' when he crashed the van.

Simon's sketchy behaviour, combined with fleeing a major crash at a police station in the middle of the day, raised some red flags. The officers searched Simon's vehicle and discovered cardboard boxes packed with 260.47 kilograms of crystal methamphetamine valued at around $130 million. In the words of Detective Inspector Glen Baker, it was 'one of the easiest drug busts that New South Wales Police have ever made'.

Simon's defence barrister said his client's actions were 'hopeless', 'negligent' and 'shambolic'. 'Shambolic is a good word,' agreed Judge Penny Hock. 'It was the offender's own incompetent or shambolic – from his own barrister's submission – driving that brought him to the attention of police.' She said the arrest was 'most unfortunate for the offender but was of great benefit to the community' and sentenced Simon to six-and-a-half years in prison.

Then there's the case of 26-year-old Sam [Redacted], who appeared before Gosford Local Court, NSW in April 2023 on one charge of supplying a prohibited drug. Sam made the unusual choice of having crystal meth posted to him in an Express Post parcel. In an amusing mix-up, his package of ice went to the wrong address and was returned to the post office. The police were alerted and the game was up. When Sam popped down to the post office a few days later to pick up *another* parcel of meth, he was arrested by a plain-clothes officer.

Magistrate Peter Miszalski wasn't messing around with words such as 'shambolic' when he gave his ruling. He told Sam he could have made a lot of money dealing meth if he hadn't been 'dumb to the extreme'. Nevertheless, his sentence was lenient. He conferred a $4000 fine rather than issuing a prison sentence. Sam was given the opportunity to start a new life – a life in which he no longer relied on Australia Post to traffic deliveries of crank.

THE CRUTCHY PUSH

AT THE TURN OF the 20th century, a standover gang known as the
Crutchy Push stalked the streets of North Melbourne. This band of
12 or so ruthless young men made their living threatening people for
money, food and booze. Between 1895 and 1905, the gang was at the
centre of countless brawls, assaults, thefts and ruckuses. They were feared
by citizens and spurned by police.

The name 'push' is an archaic Aussie slang term for 'gang'. Sydney had
plenty of pushes in its day, usually named after streets or areas, such as the
Cow Lane Push, the Gipps Street Push and the Rocks Push. Likewise,
Melbourne had the Freeman Street Push in North Fitzroy. There were
also gangs without 'push' in their titles, such as the Bouveroos, the
Irishtown Mob, the Flying Angels and the Coffin Club.

But why was this North Melbourne gang called the Crutchy Push?
A report on pushes published in *The Sydney Morning Herald* in 1953
explains the staggering reason behind the name:

> The Crutchy Push, with one exception, consisted of one-legged men.
> The exception was a one-armed man who kept half a brick in his sewn
> up empty sleeve. He led his followers into battle swinging the weighted
> sleeve around his head. Behind him came the men on crutches – each

one expert at balancing on one leg. The tip of the crutch was used to jab an opponent in the midriff. With the enemy gasping for breath the crutch would be reversed and the metal-shod arm rest would be used as a club.

I really buried the lead with this one! The Crutchy Push was an amputee-only gang whose members weaponised their crutches. It was a criminal masterclass in turning lemons into lemonade (or, in this case, turning lemons into Molotov cocktails). They were also, as the *Sunday Times* put it, 'a particularly rowdy and violent lot of ruffians'.

The push was led by William 'Valentine' Keating, a child of Irish immigrants who was first convicted of assault at the tender age of 12. It's said that Keating got the top job after his predecessor was beaten to death with an iron bar, possibly by another member of the Crutchy Push.

Keating was often in trouble with the law. In 1898 alone, he was convicted of assaulting a police officer, fined for 'insulting behaviour', sentenced to a month in prison for stealing a case of oranges and served time for stealing a pair of trousers and a mackintosh. Keating faced several charges of 'insulting behaviour' throughout his career and was convicted of assaulting a police officer no less than *eight* times. One such incident was reported in the *North Melbourne Courier and West Melbourne Advertiser* on 4 March 1898. It involved Keating and his fellow 'Crutchy' William Walsh:

Senior-Constable Healy said that on Saturday evening Walsh and Keating were creating a disturbance in Abbotsford-street. He remonstrated with them, and Walsh used bad language. Healy arrested Walsh and Keating struck witness. Witness chased Keating, but he was off like a flying kangaroo – although he goes on a crutch. Healy could not catch him, and returned, and with the assistance of Mr. Bagley, chemist, and several others, he put Walsh in a cab and took him to the lock up – Walsh struggling violently all the time. Subsequently Keating was arrested in a fish-shop in Queensberry-street.

There's also this account in the *North Melbourne Gazette* on 10 March 1899 of Keating demonstrating poor emotional regulation:

> Constable Curran said, at a quarter-past 11 on Tuesday night he went to the Commercial Hotel, Curzon-street. They demanded drink, and being refused one threw a lemonade bottle and the other a glass. Witness got assistance from Constable Noone. Keating bit [the] witness, who had to get assistance from two railway firemen to hand-cuff him. He fought like a madman, and an extra reinforcement of police had to be sent for. Altogether it took three-quarters of an hour for the police to lock the two men up.

The Age reported Constable Noone having another run-in with Keating on 3 February 1902:

> Valentine Keating ... was arrested by Constables D. McSweeney and Noone, on warrant, at North Melbourne last evening, on the charge of using obscene language. During the arrest, the prisoner, it is alleged, severely assaulted the constables by kicking them, and he has been charged with the offence. In the scuffle, another man struck one of the constables over the head with a poker, smashing his helmet, and an effort is being made to effect the offender's arrest.

Nobody could accuse Keating and the Crutchy Push of doing anything half-heartedly. On 28 August 1899, *The Argus* described a 'disgraceful scene' at a Footscray vs North Melbourne football match. During the half-time interval, 'a gang of North Melbourne roughs ... known as the "Crutchy Push", wearing bell-toppers, with blue and white streamers, attempted to push the reserve. These larrikins, after parading around, attempted to scale the fence, and were promptly ejected by the police, but not before several blows were struck.' Talk about team spirit!

The Crutchies often let their passion get the better of them as we can see in this report from Sydney's *Evening News* on 9 November 1901:

Stewart and Henry Collared, two young men, were admitted to the hospital in a cut and battered condition at 2 o'clock this morning. They stated that they were set on by five men, belonging to the notorious 'Crutchy push,' who knocked them down and kicked them. They were bruised and cut all over, and their clothing torn to pieces. The only reason given for the ferocious assault is that the push resented Stewart's claim to be the best man with his hands in North Melbourne.

What does 'the best man with his hands in North Melbourne' even mean? But the most quintessential Crutchy Push story was reported in *The Advertiser* on 18 February 1902:

Members of the notorious 'Crutchy Push' can rarely boast of two legs, but they find the substitute for the missing limb, a crutch, very handy. Yesterday Constable McSweeney was endeavoring to arrest one of the 'push,' Valentine Keating, for using obscene language, when his quarry turned and belabored him upon the head with a crutch. Keating's mother and sisters then joined in the assault on the constable ... Mrs. Keating, in an attempt to dispose of McSweeney with a chair knocked her son out instead ...

Oops! However, their tale took a dark turn when Keating, along with his girlfriend Harriet Adderley and fellow gang member John Collins, were found guilty of seriously assaulting Senior Constable Mulcahy in

September 1904. The officer was sent to remove the trio from a house they were illegally occupying. When Mulcahy arrested the squatters, Keating and Collins attacked him with their crutches while Adderley kicked him in the face. According to reports, pieces of Mulcahy's skull came unstuck during the assault.

The officer survived, but the crime dealt a massive blow to the gang. Keating and Collins were sentenced to five years in prison with hard labour. Adderley was sentenced to 12 months. Some sources suggest the loss of Keating's leadership spelt the end of the Crutchy Push. But an article published in Western Australia's *The Evening Star* in 1912 suggests otherwise: 'Melbourne has seen all its pushes pass away one by one. The Crutches alone survive. The reason is not apparent, unless it is that having their solitary leg always in motion there is none available for the police or the public to pull.'

Nobody can say for certain when the gang finally disbanded. In a way, it doesn't matter. The Crutchy Push will always be the stuff of legend.

EXCUSES, EXCUSES

THERE'S A POPULAR SAYING in the fitness community: 'Excuses are like armpits. Everyone has them and they all stink.' It's something boot camp instructors love to scream at their clients while they do push-ups in the rain.

We all make excuses and, despite what personal trainers might tell you, not all excuses 'stink'. Some are completely legit. It all depends on the context and quality of the excuse. For example:

- Valid excuse: 'I can't make boot camp because I broke my leg in four places in a skiing accident.'
- Not-so-valid excuse: 'I can't make boot camp because I'm feeling a little dehydrated and on the verge of a runny nose.'
- Invalid excuse: 'I can't make boot camp because I'm recovering from the season finale of *The Crown*.'

Then there are those excuses that defy the laws of physics and our understanding of the known universe. The following story is a case in point.

In August 2018, 54-year-old Di [Redacted] was found guilty of burglarising homes in Melbourne between 2012 and 2015. His property was searched in February 2015, where police discovered an Aladdin's cave of stolen jewellery, wallets, watches, handbags, electronics goods and cash. They also discovered a 'burglary kit' bag containing a knife, torch and wig. To top it off, Di was a match for DNA found at multiple crime scenes. The evidence was damning.

Nevertheless, Di maintained his innocence. When police confronted him with the 'burglary kit', he said it was a Halloween costume. When police said he had been spotted at several of the burgled homes, Di claimed he was inspecting properties to sell to overseas investors. According to *ABC News*, when police asked why his DNA was found at the crime scenes, he answered: 'If the DNA was there then it must have got there by magic.'

Di's excuses failed to convince law enforcement (I can't imagine why) and he was charged. He later fessed up in court and pleaded guilty. His defence lawyer explained his client had fallen into a life of crime after getting into $200,000 worth of debt with people he'd met at Crown Casino (not an ideal scenario). 'He is not some sort of master criminal,' said his lawyer. 'He's not a glamorous cat burglar. He's a middle-aged man who is drowning in debt and clumsily committed some burglaries in a manner in which he inevitably would be discovered.'

Sorcery and/or witchcraft were not mentioned.

Although Judge Susan Cohen agreed that Di's burglaries were 'not highly sophisticated', she said they still required a degree of planning and forethought. She decided a jail sentence was in order. Di would have to serve ten months in prison and a 15-month community corrections order.

No excuses.

TINY NATION, BIG TAXES

O N 31 JANUARY 2020, it was the end of an era. His Royal Highness Prince Graeme Casley formally announced the Principality of Hutt River was closing its borders after 50 years of glorious rule. The principality would no longer be issuing visas, passports or licences. The Royal Mint of Hutt River had shut up shop. The principality's Western Australian property was returning to farmland and rejoining the Commonwealth of Australia. Prince Graeme thanked the community for their 'loyal support' and 'understanding during this time'.

Before this sad announcement, the Principality of Hutt River was one of the nation's foremost 'micronations'. These so-called 'sovereign states' exist all over the world. They are typically established by individuals or groups who have declared their property (or themselves) an independent 'principality' or 'nation'. Micronations are rarely acknowledged as a 'real thing' by the international community, legal bodies or any authorities at all. Words such as 'eccentric' and 'committed' are often used to describe micronations and their founders.

Australia has produced a remarkably high number of micronations per capita. According to one source, about 30 per cent of all the micronations in the world are located Down Under! Here are some of the more well-known examples:

THE EMPIRE OF ATLANTIUM

'Atlantium' was founded by three Sydney teenagers on 27 December 1981. The 'Empire' began as a '10 square metre enclave' in the suburb of Narwee ruled over by 'His Imperial Majesty George II'. Emperor George purchased an apartment in Potts Point in 1999, which served as Atlantium's 'Imperium Proper' until 2008, when the 'capital' was relocated to the 'Province of Aurora' (a 0.76 square kilometre fenced property in the South Western Slopes region of NSW). The Empire has its own calendar system, currency, stamps, state symbols and flag. According to the Emperor, 'The purpose of Atlantium is to promote the idea ... that all human beings can and should have the right to choose their country of citizenship irrespective of where they were born or where they live.' Atlantium boasts thousands of 'citizens' from around the world. Anyone 15 years or older who can afford the US$25 processing fee can apply for citizenship through the nation's website.

THE GAY AND LESBIAN KINGDOM OF THE CORAL SEA ISLANDS

The so-called 'Gay Kingdom' was established by 'Emperor' Dale Parker Anderson on the uninhabited island of Cato, at the southern end of the Great Barrier Reef. The kingdom was founded on 14 June 2004 in response to the Australian Government's failure to recognise same-sex marriage. Emperor Dale travelled to Cato with a group of gay rights activists on a ship named *Gayflower*. He raised the rainbow flag and declared the island 'the homeland of the world's gay and lesbian peoples'. The group installed a memorial plaque honouring the occasion, set up a postal system and produced stamps and coins for sale. The kingdom was dissolved upon the legalisation of same-sex marriage in 2017.

THE PRINCIPALITY OF WY

This micronation is located at 22B Burran Avenue, Mosman, NSW. It was created following a dispute with the local council over a driveway. On 15 November 2004, 'Prince' Paul Delpart decreed in a formal ceremony that his family and their home were seceding from the municipality of Mosman (but not from NSW or Australia). In the 'Decree of Secession', Prince Paul declared the Principality of Wy 'an entity born out of individual adversity in the face of bureaucracy and politics'. Wy is known as 'The Artists' Principality' and actively supports the arts through funding and scholarships. Prince Paul and his royal family have hosted several private exhibitions at their home as well as public exhibitions held at the principality's 'embassy' in Georges Heights.

THE PROVINCE OF BUMBUNGA

On 29 March 1976, British circus trainer and uranium prospector Alec Brackstone founded the 'Province of Bumbunga' at his four-hectare farm in south-east South Australia. Brackstone was afraid Australia was on the verge of becoming a republic (he shouldn't have worried). As a staunch monarchist, he wanted to establish a 'province' to guarantee somewhere in the country would remain loyal to the Crown. He requested permission from South Australian Governor-General Sir Mark Oliphant, who apparently gave him the thumbs up. Brackstone declared himself 'Governor' and planted an enormous strawberry patch on his property in the shape of the United Kingdom. In 1980, he issued stamps featuring portraits of the Royal Family, with the omission of Duchess Sarah Ferguson (he wasn't a fan). In an interview with *The Advertiser* in 2018, 93-year-old Brackstone claimed he was still Governor of the Province. He also mentioned he wasn't overly impressed with Harry and Meghan, but that comes as no surprise.

Other worthy mentions include:

♛ *The Grand Duchy of Avram* ruled by His Eminence Prince John Charlton Rudge, the Grand Duke of Avram and Cardinal Archbishop (this sovereign state has no physical location and is steeped in the Jewish mystical philosophy of Kabbalah)

♛ *The Principality of Snake Hill* ruled by Princess Helena and her daughter Princess Paula (Princess Helena's late husband, Prince Paul, was allegedly assassinated by a sniper, but this has never been confirmed)

♛ *The Sovereign State of Aeterna Lucina* ruled by Paul Baron Neuman, Supreme Lord, Baron Neuman of Kara Bagh (this micronation gained notoriety in 1990 when land fraud charges were levelled at Supreme Lord Paul).

It's quite the colourful cast of quasi-countries and renegade royal families. But why does Australia have so many micronations? Some say it's our government's lax attitude towards secessionist sovereign states (most of the time they're just left alone). Others credit our nation's 'larrikin' spirit and history of anti-establishment sentiment. This would certainly seem to be the case when we look at the story of Leonard Casley and the Principality of Hutt River.

Leonard was born in Kalgoorlie, WA, in 1925. He served in the Royal Australian Air Force and bounced between jobs before purchasing a 75-square-kilometre wheat farm near Northampton, WA. His happy life as a farmer hit a roadblock in 1969 when the state's Wheat Board imposed strict quotas on wheat sales. Out of his 6000 acres of wheat, Leonard was only allowed to sell 100 acres worth. He was understandably miffed and made protests to the government and the Wheat Board. After these failed to make a difference, Leonard decided to take an unconventional approach.

On 21 April 1970, Leonard announced his wheat farm's secession from Australia and proclaimed himself 'His Royal Highness

Prince Leonard I of Hutt'. He notified the relevant parties, including the State Premier, the State Governor, the Acting Prime Minister and the Governor-General of Australia. The secession was never formally recognised by the State or Crown, but that wasn't going to stop Prince Leonard! He established a heraldry system, rules for royal rhetoric, a government constitution, a post office, an economic system, a non-denominational chapel, a historical society, a diplomatic security force and a 'Royal College of Advanced Research'. (According to the website, the college made mathematical discoveries 'concerning religion and pure physics ... as well as the equations for the universe at rest and the universe then "Creating".) He also set up shop selling Hutt River merchandise out of the 'Royal Mint'. This became a reasonably lucrative venture as more and more tourists stopped by to pick up their royal coins, stamps and paraphernalia.

According to Prince Leonard, his sovereign state enjoyed tax-exempt status. The Australian Taxation Office (ATO) did not agree. In 1977, Prince Leonard was fined for failing to supply the ATO with the required documents. Later that year, he briefly declared war on the Australian Government. (I'm not sure the Australian Government even knew.) His efforts to appeal the fine proved unsuccessful.

After decades of disagreement, the ATO successfully prosecuted Prince Leonard for unpaid taxes in 2006. He tried to have the ruling overturned by the High Court in 2007, but Justice Kirby and Justice Heydon ruled that 'the arguments advanced by the applicants [were] fatuous, frivolous and vexatious'. (That's a sick burn.) Prince Leonard would have to pay.

On 11 February 2017, at the age of 91, Prince Leonard abdicated his throne and passed the crown to his 60-year-old son, Prince Graeme, Duke of Gilboa, Earl of Canan, Minister of State and Education, Grand Master of the Order of Wisdom and Learning, and more. Prince Graeme hoped his rule would usher in an age of peace for the principality. 'I will be trying to bring about a more harmonious relationship with our closest neighbour, Australia, and the West Australian Government,' said the new monarch. 'We're not here as a threat.'

But dreams of friendly coexistence were short-lived. Prince Leonard was back in court four months after the abdication, defending against claims of (you guessed it) unpaid taxes! Once more, he argued that Australian tax law didn't apply to him or his sovereign state. Once more, the judge disagreed.

'Anyone can declare themselves a sovereign in their own home, but they cannot ignore the laws of Australia or not pay tax,' said Supreme Court Justice Rene Le Miere. 'It is not sensible or a proper use of judicial resources to recite and analyse all of the defendants' utterances masquerading as legal submissions. It is all gobbledygook'. (Another sick burn.)

Prince Leonard was ordered to pay the ATO a whopping $2.7 million. It was a crushing blow. Prince Graeme said the ongoing court battles had been 'mental torture' for his father.

Two years later, on 13 February 2019, Prince Leonard passed away (he was 93, so it's hard to say if his legal woes were a contributing factor). The principality closed its borders the following January and the second-biggest 'country' on the continent of Australia was gone for good.

Well, almost. Like so many micronations, the Principality of Hutt River has an *amazing* website. (Check it out – the graphics alone are worth the visit.) In fact, the website is so incredible and the story of Hutt River so remarkable that the State Library of Western Australia decided to archive it as an 'electronic publication of national significance and lasting cultural value'. After a lifetime of rebellion, who'd have guessed Prince Leonard's legacy would be preserved by a state government institution? Truly an honour worthy of royalty.

BIZARRE LAW #10

At best, weddings are a celebration of love, generosity, family and friendship. At worst, they're a portal to a dark dimension of insane drama and unspeakable horror. Countless nuptials have been ruined by mental breakdowns, unresolved family trauma, inappropriate sexual behaviour and untreated drinking problems, which is why couples should always carefully curate their guest list and have triple zero on speed dial.

We can only wonder what screwed-up ceremony inspired South Australian lawmakers to draft Section 7A of the *Summary Offences Act 1953* (SA). This law prohibits anyone from intentionally 'obstructing or disturbing' a wedding, funeral or religious service, which means no drunken heckling, practical jokes, aggressive emotional outbursts or throwing red paint on the bride's fur-lined gown. Offenders can face a hefty maximum penalty of $10,000 or two years' imprisonment, which is enough to keep any rowdy groomsmen, overbearing in-laws or disgruntled guests in check, at least until the reception gets underway.

KRISPY KRIME

A T 3.30AM ON 29 November 2023, a woman stole a white LDV van while the driver was paying for petrol at a service station in Carlington, Sydney. The van was carrying 10,000 freshly baked Krispy Kreme doughnuts (a combination of classic and Christmas-themed flavours). The theft made international news and inspired a generous sprinkling of doughnut-related puns.

NSW Police posted a statement to its Facebook page later that day with a photo of the van and its plate number. It said: 'We're on the hunt for someone who took the term "sweet getaway" to a whole new level ... if you've got any sweet leads or krispy CCTV footage, donut keep it to yourself!' Meanwhile, Krispy Kreme assured its customers it was quickly filling the hole in supply with additional doughnuts.

CBS News reported that 'detectives followed a trail of crumbs to a suburban car park, where they found the abandoned vehicle more than a week later'. The van contained thousands of spoiled, inedible doughnuts. (This must have been a horrifying scene for all police involved. We can only hope that appropriate emotional support was provided in the aftermath.)

The culprit was finally arrested and charged on 14 December 2023. By all accounts, the 28-year-old woman was likely unaware the van contained such a precious, high-calorie haul when she drove off with it. As Victor Mather of *The New York Times* wrote: 'Given that the van was unmarked, it is likely that the cargo was merely a delicious surprise to the culprit.' (It's great when a US publication that has won over 130 Pulitzer Prizes covers such noteworthy Australian stories.) The thief was refused bail, which is hardly surprising after she ruined an important source of nourishment for law enforcement officers. Talk about a sticky situation!

BIZARRE LAW #11

On 9 October 2008, Queensland State Parliament passed the *Criminal Code and Other Acts Amendment Bill*. The legislation updated Queensland's criminal code to be more reflective of modern times. For example, it was now an offence for parents or carers to abandon young children for an 'unreasonably long period' of time. (I'm surprised that wasn't a law already, but good on them for making if official.) They also removed offences they considered 'obsolete', including the law prohibiting Queenslanders from challenging opponents to a duel. As one *Brisbane Times* headline read: 'Duels OK, but mind the kids.'

The history of duelling dates back thousands of years. Ancient Romans described Germanic tribes settling disputes with one-on-one sword fights. The practice spread across Europe in the Middle Ages and became an accepted part of the medieval justice system. Judges would settle disputes by having the 'victim' and alleged 'criminal' battle it out in 'trial by combat'. If the 'accused' was successful in killing the 'accuser', they were judged innocent of the crime (the Middle Ages was freaking hardcore).

In the Renaissance, it became fashionable for gentlemen to

engage in 'duels of honour'. These were usually fought in response to an insult or hurtful remark. Challenging someone to a duel of honour was how a gentleman could 'clap back' at haters. They were usually private affairs and didn't always result in the death of the loser. Until the 18th century, duels were mainly fought with swords. After that, pistols became the popular option.

Over time, an increasing number of countries banned duels because of all the duel-related deaths and carnage. Duelling was banned in Britain in 1819 and this ban was inherited into Australian law. One by one, the Australian states and territories ditched the ban because it was deemed irrelevant. Well, all the states and territories except one.

In WA, the ban on duelling is still in full effect. Section 72 of the *Criminal Code Act Compilation Act 1913* (WA) states that 'any person who challenges another to fight a duel, or attempts to provoke another to fight a duel, or attempts to provoke any person to challenge another to fight a duel, is guilty of a crime, and liable to imprisonment for 2 years'. When I saw this, my initial reaction was to think: 'Come on WA, you're only two hours behind Queensland. It's time to get with the times!' But I was humbled to learn the WA duelling ban isn't as outmoded as I first thought. In an interview given in 2016, Senior Law Lecturer Tomas Fitzgerald confirmed there had been nine convictions for 'duel-related' offences in WA 'in the last 10 years'.

I have so many questions! Do these WA 'duellers' observe time-honoured traditions such as slapping combatants in the face with gloves or meeting at dawn with loaded pistols? Are Western Australians fighting 'duels of honour' or are duels used to settle less personal disputes, like the duel fought in Burgos, Spain in 1077 to resolve the question of whether the Mozarabic or the Roman liturgy should be used in Toledo? (In case you were wondering, the Mozarabic liturgy won the day.) Also, why are west coasters still risking their lives with in-person combat when they could just cancel their opponents on social media?

CARRY-ON CRIMINALS

WELSH-BORN BRIAN ROBSON WAS full of excitement when he flew to Australia in July 1964. The Australian Government had sponsored the 18-year-old to relocate from Cardiff to Melbourne and work as a ticket inspector for Victorian Railways. It sounded like the adventure of a lifetime!

But life as a ticket inspector didn't prove as thrilling as he'd hoped (no shit, Sherlock), and Brian struggled to fit in. He longed to be back in Wales but couldn't afford the airfare (ticket inspector wages weren't exactly 'balling'). Desperate to return home, the Welshman concocted a daring plan.

According to *The Age*, Brian purchased a crate large enough for him to squeeze into with his knees pressed up against his chest (you can see where this is going). He booked the crate to be transported from Melbourne to London by air. With the help of two friends, he packed himself inside, along with some 'essentials', including water, a hammer, a pillow, a flashlight and a book of Beatles songs. There's nothing like reading the lyrics to 'I Want to Hold Your Hand' while travelling 16,000 kilometres in a wooden crate. To guarantee the precious cargo was handled with care, the crate was labelled 'Ajax Computer' and 'this way up'. Brian's friends checked one last time that he was sure he wanted to do this, nailed the box shut and loaded it onto a truck going to Melbourne Airport.

Brian should have landed in London 36 hours later. But, as so often happens with international postage, things didn't go according to plan. When the crate arrived in Sydney, handlers turned the box upside down and left it that way for 23 hours. So much for the 'this way up' sign. It was finally flipped right-side up when it was loaded onto the next plane. Sadly for Brian, this wasn't a Qantas flight from Sydney to London. The package had been diverted and was now on a Pan Am flight to Los Angeles.

Of course, conditions in the box were less than ideal. As well as being incredibly cramped, the temperature in the crate fluctuated from very cold to very hot. Brian spilt his water early in the trip and was suffering the effects of dehydration. 'You're going in and out of consciousness the whole time,' he told *The New York Times*, 'you're having very weird dreams and you're not sure whether the dreams are real.' His voyage home had turned into a bad acid trip.

Brian had been in the box for over three days when a freight worker at Los Angeles Airport noticed a light shining from inside the 'Ajax Computer' crate. The worker peeked inside and discovered a human being! Brian was quickly unpacked and rushed to the prison ward of Los Angeles County General Hospital. He was a bit worse for wear but didn't sustain any lasting physical injuries.

Brian was in trouble with Australian *and* American authorities for illegally smuggling himself across international borders. He was held for three months while law enforcement deliberated.

During this time, a spokesperson for the Australian immigration department made a statement addressing the incident. 'Due to his unsatisfactory record in his short time in Australia, and as there seemed little prospect of his successful settlement, Robson was to be offered repatriation to Wales,' he said. 'Before this decision was conveyed to him he apparently left Australia. Had he reported to the department ... as he should have done, Robson would now be home in Wales.' Oops!

Australian and American authorities ended up taking mercy on Brian and dropped all charges. He wasn't a threat; his crime was kind of pathetic and he'd suffered enough. He was released and bundled on a plane to London, free of charge. He went on to write a book about his misadventures entitled *The Crate Escape*, so I guess it wasn't a total failure.

Another example of why packing yourself into a crate isn't a good idea was reported by *The Age* on 22 September 1982. A gang of five men closely connected with the Painters and Dockers Union attempted to steal $600,000 in cash from the Commonwealth Bank. Four of the gang members were packed into individual shipping crates and boarded onto TAA flights out of Brisbane. The flights were carrying crates of money destined for bank branches in Cairns, Mt Isa, Rockhampton and Townsville.

The plan was for each of the men to switch the money mid-flight with telephone books they had packed in their crates with them. That way the handlers wouldn't notice the weight discrepancy in the bank's crates until it was too late. Unfortunately for the Mt Isa–bound thief, he couldn't locate the money because his crate was packed into the wrong section of the cargo locker. Worse still, the Rockhampton-bound robber *nearly died* because his crate was packed into a low-oxygen area of the hold. As for the Cairns-bound criminal, his crate was accidentally left behind at a Brisbane Eagle Farm Airport cargo depot.

The word 'shemozzle' springs to mind.

Police were alerted to the heist and greeted the robbers at gunpoint. Force wasn't required when it came to arresting the Rockhampton robber. According to *The Age*, 'the man appeared to be extremely sick and cramped and was in no condition to escape'. The five gang members were caught and the money was recovered. Assistant Police Commissioner

Tony Murphy called it 'the most brazen and bizarre robbery attempt' he had ever seen.

But we shouldn't exclusively focus on people packing themselves into crates on planes. After all, air travel isn't the only option for stupid stowaways who want to illegally risk their lives.

In 2023, an intoxicated 43-year-old man (let's call him 'Cameron') hitched a ride by secretly crawling onto the metal gate racks beneath a B-double trailer truck that had stopped at Nambucca Heads on the North Coast of NSW. He planned to make the 32-minute journey to Coffs Harbour and get off when the truck stopped at a red light. But there must have been a run of green lights, because the truck didn't stop until they reached the Gold Coast suburb of Tugun, 340 kilometres north of Nambucca Heads.

According to *ABC News*, the driver noticed a piece of orange cloth under the trailer and went to investigate. He was surprised to see a full-grown man clambering out from underneath. Cameron was extremely apologetic. (I'm guessing the booze had started to wear off.) The driver gave him some water and offered him a seat in the truck. They drove another 50 kilometres north before stopping at a service station in Coomera. That's when the driver called the cops.

Cameron received a $288 fine and a ride to Coomera railway station. Queensland Trucking Association chief executive Gary Mahon said Cameron was 'an extremely fortunate person to have travelled [that distance] and still be okay at the end'. He 'strongly discouraged' anyone from clinging to the bottom of trucks as a mode of transport, which is excellent advice.

UNHOLY HIJINKS

ON 14 FEBRUARY 1945, 36-year-old Max Wannerstrom was intercepted at the Holy Trinity Church in Brisbane. He was wearing a
black silk clerical gown and black gloves. But Max wasn't a priest. He
was a scurrilous 'seaman' from Denmark with a taste for liquor.

According to *The Northern Miner* newspaper, Max snuck into the
church with the intention of stealing communion wine. The church
caretaker potted the intruder and confronted him, but Max struck him
in the right eye and carried on with the robbery. The caretaker called
the police, who arrived just in time to catch Max leaving the church.
When they asked him what he was doing, 'he claimed he was the assistant rector and was searching for a man who had done damage inside
the church'. It was a good effort, but the jig was up when the caretaker
identified Max as the culprit. He was fined £17 (equivalent to A$1490),
ordered to pay restitution of £7 and sentenced to three months in prison.
The Northern Miner failed to mention why Max had a clerical gown in
the first place (I wonder if he was into some kinky role-play?).

Another church-related theft was reported in Sydney's *Daily Mirror*
on 9 October 1946. Twenty-nine-year-old Morris Parkes, 30-year-old
George Sutton and 31-year-old Stanley Burcher were charged with
breaking and entering All Saint's Church in Parramatta and 'stealing

religious articles valued at £10'. A priest's surplice, cassock and cape were stolen after the group of friends decided to conduct a 'mock wedding' (as you do). Detective JB Renehan busted their party at 3.30am on 3 September 1946. He discovered Morris 'wearing a white surplice, with a cassock over his shoulder'. Renehan reported 'empty bottles and broken eggs strewn about the house'. (The fake nuptials must have really kicked off.) The jury found George and Stanley guilty. They were fined £500 each (equivalent to A$43,000) and put on good behaviour bonds. Morris was found not guilty and discharged (not sure why, but good for him!).

Police were 'puzzled' by a robbery at a Roman Catholic church in Woodville Gardens, Adelaide on 8 April 1952. According to *The Advertiser*, thieves gained entry through a smashed window and made off with 'two large candlesticks, candles and church vestments, a large wooden crucifix and a small wooden cross'. Nothing else was stolen, which begs the question *why*? Was it another 'mock wedding', a pilfering rival church or devil-worshippers stealing supplies for a satanic mass? I couldn't find any follow-up reports, so I'll leave this one to the reader's unholy imagination.

Seventy years later, Greek Orthodox churches in Melbourne were plagued by burglaries in an 'Easter crime spree'. On 25 April 2022, *Nine News* reported that a 45-year-old man had been arrested after no less than ten churches were robbed. CCTV caught footage of a thief sneaking into a Saturday service at St Haralambos Greek Orthodox Church in Templestowe and making off with a donation bowl carrying $300. *Nine News* interviewed George Papadopoulos of St Nicholas Greek Orthodox Church in Yarraville, which was also burglarised. 'Go and confess!' said George, addressing the thief. 'For what you have done ... you're going to be judged!' And George was correct. The thief – 46-year-old Stipo [Redacted] of Caroline Springs – was judged at Sunshine Magistrates' Court in March 2023. Stipo faced charges of theft from several churches, as well as stealing approximately $300 from a Thai Buddhist church in Mont Albert (bad karma). Magistrate Michael McNamara ordered Stipo to pay compensation of $770. Stipo thanked the magistrate for showing him leniency. 'From the bottom of my heart, I won't do any more crime and won't do any more time,' he said. For the sake of his immortal soul, let's hope he's true to his word.

LOVE ME SAILOR

LOVE ME SAILOR BY Melbourne-born author Robert Close landed in Australian bookstores in 1945. The blurb read as follows:

> An authentic narrative of early convict days. What happens when a sexually active female is a passenger on board a sailing vessel with a crew of lawless men.
>
> The author's first novel, dealing with the voyage of a windjammer and the chaos caused on board by its sole passenger, a neurotic nymphomaniac.

It should come as no surprise that a book published in the 1940s about a 'neurotic nymphomaniac' stuck at sea with a 'crew of lawless men' was hit with obscenity charges in multiple states. It was inevitable.

The Crown Prosecutor in the South Australian case didn't enjoy the novel. When addressing the Adelaide Police Court on 9 July 1946, RR Chamberlain launched into a blistering tirade worthy of a *Comedy Central* roast:

> The author has dragged his talents through the mud, and no artistic work could justify the book's filth.

The book ends on page 261 – which is 261 pages too late for decent-minded people ...

I've read the book carefully, and marked numerous filthy passages which appear typical of its contents. However, the highlight of indecency seems to have been reached with Close's description of the second mate taking a cabin boy on his first visit to a Paris brothel. Here, absolutely nothing is left to the imagination.

I shudder to think of the impression this book would make on young minds. Frankly, it left me with a feeling of nausea ...

Close and his publisher, Georgian House Pty Ltd, also faced charges of 'obscene libel' at the Supreme Court of Victoria in 1946. To convey the novel's full 'obscenity', the entire 90,000-word book was read aloud to the jury. But there was a mistrial when it was discovered that the foreperson of the jury had discussed the case with an acquaintance of Close. They had to hold a second trial and read the entire book aloud *again*. (The mental image of a full courtroom listening to an uptight prosecutor read aloud the scene about the 'cabin boy on his first visit to a Paris brothel' fills me with indescribable joy.)

Proceedings didn't wrap up until April 1948 when the defendants were found guilty and Close was sentenced to three months in prison and given a £100 fine (equivalent to A$7500). Authors and literary society officials protested as the writer was dragged away in handcuffs. Thankfully, the sentence was reduced on appeal to ten days in prison (which is still ten days too many in this humble author's opinion).

Close moved to Paris in 1950. He went on to write four more novels, but none gained him the same notoriety as *Love Me Sailor*, which he called 'his old albatross'. In an interview with *The Age* in 1961, Close said he still enjoyed 'puncturing the pompous and the prudish, and those warped types who try to put sin into sex'. *Vive la résistance!*

WHO STOLE THOSE TEETH?

IN RESEARCHING THIS BOOK, I stumbled upon a surprising number of early-to-mid-20th-century newspaper articles reporting the theft of false teeth. I'm not talking about random burglars stealing someone's dentures (although that did happen, because people are weird). The articles in question describe thieves running off with many false teeth. In one case, a Canberra dentist reportedly lost up to 30,000 false teeth in a single heist. That's quite a haul!

False teeth were often made with valuable materials such as gold or porcelain, which goes some way to explaining the phenomenon, but not all the way. Some reports describe the thefts as 'curious' or 'strange', which would suggest tooth theft wasn't the type of crime people of the era expected. So what the hell was going on?

I have nothing to add that could improve the entertainment value of these reports, so here's a selection for you to enjoy:

'WHO STOLE THOSE TEETH? A Curious Theft. False Teeth Galore.' *The Express and Telegraph* (Adelaide, SA), 28 June 1905
'There are some people who would steal anything,' a detective remarked to a representative of *The Advertiser* a day or two ago. This remark was prophetic as on Wednesday morning Mr. H. Mallan had occasion

to exclaim, 'Who stole my teeth?' Mr. Mallan practises as a dentist in King William-street near the Gresham Hotel, and on Tuesday afternoon when he left his rooms everything was right, but the next morning everything was wrong. Two showcases in front of the premises had been broken open, and hundreds of teeth in the form of upper sets, lower sets, gold teeth, teeth with gold filling, teeth mounted on porcelain gums, and some heavy American crown and bridge work executed in gold had been taken. Mr. Mallan stated that £200 would not repay him for the loss as among the stolen property was a quantity of work which had gained for him medals at exhibitions in London, Vienna, and Paris. When the Sultan of Johore visited Adelaide some time ago the sight of his dazzling teeth endowed Mr. Mallan with a desire to engage in setting diamonds in teeth. There was a piece of this kind of work valued at about £10 in one of the showcases, but, strange to say, the thief did not appropriate this, and he also neglected to take some pure gold work. As the thief took the trouble to carry away a number of sets of vulcanite work the idea is suggested that he must have some reason to expect that he can dispose of them to some dentist to use as exhibition work, because it has no other commercial use. The padlocks to the showcases were forced open, and this morning one of the padlocks was found lying on the ground beneath the cases. The detectives are already investigating the matter, and as the thief cannot possibly use more than one set at a time he will probably seek to dispose of the remainder. Mr. Mallan is willing to give a substantial reward for the conviction of the teeth-stealer.

'THEFT OF FALSE TEETH.' *The Telegraph* **(Brisbane, Qld), 6 July 1917**

David Henry Brewer, 26, engineer, was charged in the City Police

Court yesterday, before Mr. W. Harris, P.M., ... on 11th July, at Brisbane, he stole 42 false teeth, valued at £7 7s., the property of Charles Garnet Genn.

Sergeant Bell prosecuted.

The accused pleaded guilty.

Sergeant Bell said that Mr. Genn was a dentist in Queen street, and the accused went into his surgery in connection with his own teeth. While there he stole the teeth. Mr. Genn informed the police, and the accused, after giving considerable trouble, pulled the teeth out of his pocket, and tried to get away from the police.

Accused said that his action was done more out of spite than anything else.

The P.M. sentenced accused to two months' imprisonment, sentence to be suspended upon accused entering his own bond of £60 to be of good behaviour for 12 months.

'300 FALSE TEETH: Alleged Theft.' *The Sun* **(Sydney, NSW), 16 March 1918**

MELBOURNE, Saturday – Clarence Prescott Hannah, a soldier, was charged at the City Court to-day with having stolen 300 false teeth from Felton, Grimwade, and Co. He was remanded.

'THEFT OF FALSE TEETH.' *Moree Gwydir Examiner and General Advertiser* **(Moree, NSW), 22 November 1923**

Thieves forced the door of the premises of M. S. Sowerley, dental importer, Collins Street, Melbourne, and stole 700 false teeth, valued at £76.

🦷

'3000 FALSE TEETH STOLEN.' *The Richmond River Express and Casino Kyogle Advertiser* **(Casino, NSW), 13 August 1929**

Mystery surrounds the whereabouts of 3000 false teeth, valued at £900, which were in the cabin trunks of Dr. P. Koonin, a dentist, and a passenger on the Hobsons Bay for Melbourne. Dr. Koonin wished to break his voyage at Colombo, as he had entered into partnership with another dentist passenger with a practice there. The trunks were found to be cut open, and the teeth, insured for £975, gone. Detectives at Fremantle made further inquiries, but were unsuccessful.

🦷

'STRANGE THEFT: Thousands of False Teeth.' *The Canberra Times* **(Canberra, ACT), 1 July 1931**

MELBOURNE, Tuesday. Thieves, who entered the offices of the Unsworth Dental Supplies of Australasia, Ltd., in Collins Street, stole dental materials valued at more than £800.

Included among the articles stolen were between 25,000 and 30,000 false teeth.

🦷

'16,000 TEETH STOLEN. Strange Robbery in Sydney.' *The Courier-Mail* **(Brisbane, Qld), 20 September 1933**

SYDNEY, September 19. Thieves who broke into the premises of the Commonwealth Dental Supply Co., in Bathurst Street, city, during the week-end took only artificial teeth of the best grade, valued at about £500.

The thieves forced a door, and made their way into the company's showroom by cutting through a fibre partition, and then ransacked a cabinet, taking about 16,000 teeth. Other teeth of quality and valuable dental equipment were not touched.

'THEFT OF 14,000 FALSE TEETH: CHARGE AGAINST LABOURER.' *Western Argus* **(Kalgoorlie, WA), 24 April 1934**

Sydney, April 18. Osmond Robert MacLachlan (52), labourer, was charged at the Central Police Court to-day with having stolen 14,000 artificial teeth after having broken and entered the warehouse of the Commonwealth Dental Supply Co., Ltd., Bathurst street, Sydney, about September 16, 1933. He was also charged with having, at Leichhardt, on April 17 1934, had in his custody 830 artificial teeth, suspected of having been stolen.

Mr. Gibson, S.M., remanded McLachlan to April 27.

'500 FALSE TEETH STOLEN.' *The Daily Telegraph* **(Sydney, NSW), 26 June 1937**

CASINO, Friday. Five hundred false teeth were stolen early today from G. J. Mortimer's dental surgery. Recently a quantity of fine gold used for fillings and a gold watch were stolen from the same surgery.

'Stole 831 False Teeth.' *The Advertiser* **(Adelaide, SA), 17 November 1954**

PERTH, Nov. 16. A salesman stole 831 false teeth over the past six months from the medical warehouse where he was employed.

He also took six electric shavers, some cash and toilet goods.

The value of his thefts totalled £400.

In Perth Police Court today, the salesman, 22-year-old Jack Ernest Young, of Bayswater, was sentenced to 12 months' gaol.

You now know as much as I do about the history of false tooth theft in Australia between 1905 and 1954. I can only hope a historian with a penchant for dental research will one day shed more light on the matter (shout-out to any history PhD candidates hunting for a thesis topic!). It's one hell of a mystery to masticate over.

BIZARRE LAW #12

When something valuable is lost or stolen, the only thing most people want is to get it back. Once your wedding ring, Birkin bag or limited-edition Baby Yoda toy is back where it belongs, who cares what happened? *Que sera, sera.*

Early 20th-century Western Australian lawmakers weren't so forgiving. Under Section 138 of the *Criminal Code Compilation Act 1913* (WA), it is an offence to publicly offer a reward for the return of any stolen or lost property with the promise that you won't ask questions or take legal action against the individual returning the property. Failure to comply can result in a fine of up to $2000.

Warning west coasters: if someone returns your stolen property, you *better* ask questions, and you *better* take legal action. Don't let thieves off the hook!

HOW DARE YOU

W E'VE ALL HEARD STORIES of celebrities behaving badly on planes. Like when supermodel Naomi Campbell lost her cool on a British Airways jet and attacked two police officers over a lost bag. Or the time actor Alec Baldwin was kicked off an American Airlines flight at Los Angeles Airport because he refused to stop playing 'Words with Friends' on his phone. Or the time not-quite-first-lady Ivana Trump hurled abuse at a group of children on a Delta Airways flight and told the cabin crew to 'fuck off'. Or the time French movie star Gerard Depardieu publicly urinated on the cabin floor of an Air France flight (when you gotta go, you gotta go). Things get messy when the stars hit the sky.

But it's not only celebrities who act the fool on flights. Australian bank executive Thomas [Redacted] gave Naomi Campbell a run for her money when he went full diva mode on a Qantas flight from Auckland to Sydney in 2020. The 39-year-old had obviously downed a few too many in-flight beverages when he began pestering a man seated in front of him. When passengers were asked to turn off their electronic devices or put them in flight mode, Thomas phoned a friend and enjoyed an extremely audible conversation. According to *The Daily Mail*, flight attendants repeatedly asked Thomas to stay seated, but he kept getting up, saying he 'needed to piss'. The pilot alerted police to the passenger's star-quality behaviour.

Thomas was greeted by a blue-and-white-striped welcoming committee when the plane landed at Sydney Airport. He was less than impressed. 'How dare you,' he said to the officers. 'I can't believe this is Australia, am I under arrest?'

Spot on! He was indeed under arrest. Thomas unsuccessfully attempted to kick two officers as they pushed him to the ground, hurting one officer's thumb in the process. 'You have no idea who I am,' he said. 'You don't realise how big a mistake you've just made ... You're gone. I'm taking your badge.' (Hot tip: don't tell a police officer mid-arrest you're going to 'take their badge'. They don't like it.)

'You've just fucked up,' he told the arresting officers. But it was Thomas who had fucked up. As the effects of the alcohol wore off, the banker apologised to the officer injured in the scuffle. 'I'm really sorry,' he said. 'I had a few drinks.' That much was obvious.

Thomas pled guilty to obstructing an officer and failing to comply with crew instructions. Magistrate Jennifer Atkinson sentenced him to a $1000 fine and a two-year good behaviour bond, which was quite lenient, all things considered. (Naomi Campbell was sentenced to 200 hours of community service for her airport police brawl.) His real punishment came when he faced the bank board. They opted to reduce his salary following the incident. For a bank executive, that's a harsh penalty indeed. No new Mercedes for Thomas.

BIZARRE LAW #13

Section 58B of the *Summary Offences Act 1953* (SA) prohibits the sale or hire of a refrigerator, ice chest or ice box over 42.5 litres unless it can be opened easily from the inside. It is also an offence to dispose of a refrigerator, ice chest or ice box over 42.5 litres at 'any dump, tip, sanitary depot, public reserve, public place or unfenced vacant land' unless all the doors and lids or locks and hinges have been removed. Fridge felons can face fines of up to $750.

This law comes from an era when fridges posed a much greater threat to public safety than they do today. In the mid-20th century, it was not unheard of for people to get locked inside refrigerators. That is why the law limits fridge size unless anyone trapped inside can easily free themselves. But I have no idea why SA was the only state to enshrine this policy in legislation. Did it have an unusually high number of ice box incidents? Was Adelaide the fridge-fatality capital of Australia? It's a white goods mystery for the ages.

Fortunately, South Australians on the market for high-capacity cold storage don't need to worry about breaking the law.

Almost all modern refrigerators have magnetic seal doors that can be opened from the inside. This makes it perfectly legal for SA residents to pick up a 690-litre frost-free stainless steel four-door fridge at their local appliances store. Ice cream for everyone!

INFERIOR THEFT AUTO

I F YOU'RE GOING TO steal a car, you should at least know how to drive the car you're stealing. In fact, I would say it's essential to the entire car-stealing process.

On 4 May 2021, two men learned this lesson the hard way when they tried to steal a Hyundai i30 in Bentleigh, Melbourne. The thieves threatened the car's owner with a knife outside his home at 3.30am. They took his keys and wallet but were disappointed to discover he didn't have any cash. The men decided to drive the owner to an ATM but ran into a snag when they discovered the Hyundai was a manual. Neither knew how to drive a manual and stalled the car several times. Eventually, the thieves gave up and ran away empty-handed.

This is what we call an 'epic fail'.

Earlier in 2021, footage of another car theft gone awry went viral on Reddit. The video shows an unnamed man (let's call him Brayden) behind the wheel of a white Mitsubishi Outlander at a dealership in Brisbane. Brayden was attempting to steal the vehicle but couldn't turn on the switch-button handbrake. Dealership staff surrounded the car, but Brayden locked the doors before they could get in (props to Brayden for knowing how to lock the doors).

When Brayden finally got the Mitsubishi going, he tried to swing a

U-turn but ran into a curb. A posse of dealership staff surrounded the car, shouting 'get out of the car, mate'. A Toyota LandCruiser blocked his exit, but Brayden refused to budge. A staffer got the car open by smashing the driver's side window with a steel bollard. Brayden was wrestled to the ground, screaming 'help me' and 'I wasn't taking it'. (I get the impression Brayden bit off more than he could chew.) There are no confirmed reports of what happened next, but it's safe to assume Brayden spent some quality time with the cops.

A BIT OF BAD LUCK

For millennia, the Anangu people have venerated Uluru as a resting place for ancestral spirits. Important ceremonies are held there, and the Anangu people have protocols for how to behave in the presence of this sacred monument.

Of course, these ancient beliefs and customs were completely ignored by European settlers. Tourists began visiting the area in 1936 and a chain was erected on the site in 1963 to help visitors climb to the top (which is strictly forbidden under Indigenous lore). The Australian Government took a step in the right direction in 1985 when they returned ownership of the land to the Anangu people. But the arrangement still allowed tourists to climb the monument. This gave a 25-year-old French woman the opportunity to do a striptease on top of the sacred site in 2010, calling her actions 'a tribute to the greatness of the rock'. Football 'personality' Sam Newman was photographed hitting a gold ball off Uluru the same year (not everyone is blessed with their fair share of brain cells). These acts of blatant disrespect caused significant outrage, and climbing Uluru was officially banned in October 2019.

But there are other options for sightseers who want to flaunt their ignorance and/or stupidity. Stealing souvenirs is a time-honoured tourist tradition and many visitors pocket pieces of Uluru to take home with them. Needless to say, robbing rocks is frowned upon by the Anangu people. As one traditional owner advised: 'It's fine if you take a photo of this place and take that away ... but leave the rocks.' It's also illegal to remove rocks, sand or soil from the area. The offence carries a maximum fine of $5000.

Hundreds of stolen rocks are mailed back to Uluru-Kata Tjuta National Park's main office every year. These so-called 'sorry rocks' are dispatched from all over the world and are often sent with messages of remorse. The following note was included in a 'sorry rock' parcel sent in July 2003: 'Many years ago (1988) our family visited Uluru and collected these pieces of the rock. We have all had pangs of guilt ever since could you please return these to their rightful place.'

Good for them. It took 15 years, but they got there in the end! Here's another apology message from September 2003:

> Whilst visiting Uluru last year my boyfriend took a rock. I was not happy about it, and after nearly a year of persuading, I have managed to get him to let me send it back ... I do hope not everyone is as stupid as my boyfriend – otherwise Uluru will be rapidly decreasing in size!

Sure, your 'boyfriend' stole the rock – cool story.

But guilt isn't the only motivating factor when it comes to returning rocks. As we can see in this message from 2000, some visitors claim to have fallen under a 'curse' after stealing from Uluru: 'I believe that my family is experiencing a lot of ill health and bad luck since then and although people may laugh at my superstitious nature I believe the stones are something to do with this.'

The 'Uluru curse' isn't part of the Anangu people's lore, but many visitors believe returning the stolen rocks is the only way to turn their luck around. As Park Manager Brooke Watson told *The Age* in 2003, 'we stack [the rocks] in boxes, and every now and then we try and return them to (Uluru) so that people's bad luck is dissolved'. Some people spend a good deal of money on lifting their curses, such as one visitor who posted back a 7.5-kilogram stone from Germany in 2002. I wonder if they wrote 'cursed object' on the customs declaration form.

But not everyone relies on the postal system to get the job done. Canberra resident Steve [Redacted] drove over 2500 kilometres to hand-deliver the rock he'd taken on a camping trip in 2017. He told his daughters about the geological memento after the trip, and they said he should return it right away. He didn't listen (typical) and was soon plagued by a 'run of bad luck'. The 'Uluru curse' proved particularly damaging to Steve's four wheel drive, which had to undergo $13,000 in repairs following a string of accidents and a blown-up engine. He started to believe his bad fortune was 'more than just coincidence' when photos from his Uluru trip mysteriously disappeared from his phone. Steve confessed to *Australian Geographic* that he was 'a complete idiot for taking [the rock] in the first place' and made a pilgrimage back to the national park in June 2018. He reported feeling like a weight had been lifted off his shoulders when he returned the piece of sacred land to its rightful home.

If you're one of the 500,000 tourists who visit Uluru every year, please keep it classy. If you want a souvenir, you can always pop into the Aboriginal-owned Ininti Cafe at the Uluru-Kata Tjuta Cultural Centre and peruse their selection of 'books, clothes, bags, jewellery, traditional bush medicine and other beautiful gifts'. That way you can purchase a fabulous keepsake *and* support the traditional owners, without running the risk of a $5000 fine or inflicting misfortune on yourself or your loved ones. That's what we call a 'win-win'.

AUTO-ABDUCTION

FAME IS FLEETING. IT'S a constant battle to remain relevant in the cutthroat world of entertainment. Some performers will do almost anything to draw the public's eye. Who could forget Kim Kardashian's 72-day marriage, Charlie Sheen's 'tiger blood' rant or Anna Nicole Smith's drunken speech at the 2004 Billboard Awards? Then there's Kanye West, but I don't have the word count to cover every example of him clambering for attention.

On 15 December 1991, Gold Coast nightclub singer Fairlie Arrow disappeared from her home in Surfers Paradise. Concerns immediately arose that she had been abducted by an obsessed fan. Fairlie had reportedly been stalked for months by an unnamed man who had broken into her home several times. He had allegedly done creepy stuff, such as moving around the furniture, laying out her lingerie on the bed and writing messages in lipstick on the bathroom mirror. It was all very Glenn Close in *Fatal Attraction*.

Fairlie's husband, George, spoke at a press conference and pleaded for the safe return of his wife. 'She always told me about this man and it seemed like he was in love with her,' he said, almost in tears. 'If this man cares for her then he'll let her go. I can understand why he's done it – she's beautiful. It will be the best Christmas present if she comes home to us.'

Auto-abduction

His Christmas miracle came sooner than expected. On 17 December, Fairlie was found unharmed on the side of the road. She claimed her kidnapper had 'dumped' her there, but police were unconvinced. Suspicions arose when a cleaner reported seeing Fairlie chillaxing at a nearby motel during the two-day 'ordeal'.

Fairlie maintained her innocence. The 27-year-old was adamant she had been kidnapped, gagged, blindfolded and tied to a four-poster bed. The singer described it as 'the most frightening experience of my life'. She assured anyone doubting her story: 'Trust me. This is not a bad publicity stunt.'

Two weeks later, Fairlie admitted it was a bad publicity stunt. Her career was on the slide prior to the 'abduction'. How better to revive her flailing profile than a spot of false imprisonment? She had pulled off the hoax with the support of her associate, 'Big Bob' Deering (a panelbeater known for his lavish lifestyle and elaborate gold jewellery). What could possibly go wrong?

None too pleased, the police sent Fairlie a bill for $18,000 to compensate for the wasted search. They also charged her with making a false complaint and false statement. George filed for divorce shortly afterwards (I think we all understand why).

SIGN OF THE CRIMES

On 13 February 2019, *Vice* published an article by radio presenter Marty Smiley titled 'The True Story of How the Parramatta Road Sign Ended Up in Lebanon'. The article outlined Smiley's mission to answer the question: 'What kind of legend steals a sign, flies it across the planet, then bolts it to a power pole in a remote village in Lebanon?' (It's a fair question.)

Smiley was intrigued by a photo of a Parramatta Road sign erected in the sparsely populated Lebanese village of Kfarsghab. He was travelling in Lebanon and decided to visit the misplaced sign for himself. He asked the locals about the strange landmark, but nobody knew how the sign had made the 14,000-kilometre journey from Western Sydney or who was responsible for stealing it. Smiley ended up calling Jennifer Hanna, Secretary of the Australian Kfarsghab Association. She told him the sign had been there since 1995 and was a gift from Parramatta City Council to the people of Kfarsghab. The gift was made 'to honour the 20,000-plus Kfarsghab descendants living in Australia, and particularly Parramatta'. It remained a 'lasting symbol of the connection between Lebanon and Australia'.

Turns out there was no crime committed and no thief to find. But in fairness to Smiley, he had every reason to suspect the sign was stolen.

It's a common crime and Aussie pranksters love to have fun with street signage.

In 2013, *The Canberra Times* reported a case of public sign shenanigans from 1962. The article referred to a report published by *The Canberra Times* on 21 February 1962, titled 'SPELLING TO BE EXAMINED'. This report covered a parliamentary exchange over an apparently misspelt signpost:

> Mis-spelling on a Constitution Avenue signpost would be examined, the Minister for the Interior, Mr. Freeth, promised last night.
>
> Member for the A.C.T., Mr. J. R. Fraser, had drawn his attention in the House of Representatives to the mis-spelling.
>
> The signpost mistakenly spelt it 'Constipation Avenue,' he said.
>
> Mr. Fraser asked the Minister to have the signpost re-moved and replaced with a correctly spelt sign.

'Constipation Avenue' – talk about a backed-up road! But the 'misspelt' sign wasn't an innocent mistake. It was a prank pulled off by a posse of pals. One of the pranksters, Graham Yapp, told *The Canberra Times* the original plan was to change 'Constitution' to 'Prostitution', but they decided against it for fear of causing offence. Toilet humour prevailed, and for a brief, shining moment, 'Constipation Avenue' intersected Coranderrk Street in the Australian capital. It was a magical time in our national history.

Before I go any further, I want to state that stealing or defacing public signs is illegal and potentially dangerous. The author does not endorse any kind of unauthorised interference with government property. That said, this next case of public vandalism really warms my heart.

On 31 May 2013, the *Eastern Courier Messenger* reported a street sign vandal at work in the inner-eastern Adelaide suburbs of Norwood, Kensington Park and Beulah Park. The undercover artist was busy transforming stop signs into messages of love and hope, including 'Don't STOP Dreaming', 'I Just Can't STOP Lovin' You' and 'Nothing's Gonna STOP Us Now'. The local council was none too pleased. It had replaced four altered stop signs to date, and Mayor Robert Bria said the signs had 'the potential to divert drivers' attention away from the road and cause accidents'.

However, local cafe owner Daniel Milky expressed admiration for the creative endeavour. 'I think it's great,' he said. 'The idea is trying to get people to take notice of what's going on around them.' Mr Milky believed the same street artist was responsible for a picture that appeared on the outside wall of his cafe depicting US President Theodore 'Teddy' Roosevelt made up of Tiny Teddies (which sounds amazing). The article reminded readers that the fine for defacing council property is $187, no matter how joyful or inspiring the artwork might be.

But not all public sign crimes are humorous or life-affirming. Some are driven by the darkest impulses of the human soul.

A particularly egregious case was reported by *The Herald Sun* on 28 May 2019. A fake 'no parking' sign was erected on a residential street in Craigieburn, Melbourne. One local speculated that it was the work of a resident who disliked people parking in their street, but nobody knew who was responsible. The sign was convincing enough for local law enforcement to issue hundreds of dollars in illegitimate fines. (I swear, the perpetrator of this offence is one of the most malicious and mean-spirited criminals in this book. What kind of spiritually bankrupt individual would betray their fellow drivers by landing them with fake parking fines?) Victoria Police had reimbursed five victims of the hoax and were on the hunt for anyone else deserving of a refund. At the time of reporting, the sign had been removed by a person or persons unknown. The horror of Craigieburn's faux parking sign was gone but never forgotten.

Another dastardly public sign crime was perpetrated on 8 October 2020 in the western Queensland town of Tambo. Thieves made off with two novelty signs erected to protect the welfare of local teddy bears. The yellow-and-black signs cautioned drivers to be careful of teddies crossing Arthur Street near the town's top teddy bear shop, Tambo Teddies. The store's co-owner, Alison Shaw, told *ABC News* the signs were 'iconic' (which is a word I usually reserve for the likes of Beyoncé, but okay). Alison published a post titled 'We're a bit Cross about the Crossing Signs' (harsh words indeed) on the Tambo Teddies website. The post included this poem written by 'De Baggis', a fan of the store:

If you go into Tambo today
You're in for a big surprise
Cos all the teddy bear signs there was
Are all now gone because
A thieving person did nick them!

It's not exactly Robert Frost, but I admire the conviction. Online commenters were outraged by the heinous crime and raised concerns for the safety of Tambo's teddies. As one Facebook commenter remarked: 'How are the Teddies going to know where the safe road crossing is??? Imagine if you were a Teddy and someone took away the signs for your crossing! How would you feel?'

Thankfully, two replacement signs were donated two weeks later, and the teddies of Tambo were safe again to head out for picnics (or pop down to the Tambo Tavern for a couple of cold ones). The new signs were 'bigger and better' than the last and secured with 'theft-proof bolts'. It was a total upgrade.

But 'theft-proof bolts' aren't the only solution for decreasing public sign crime. After a spate of sign thefts in the WA region of Pilbara, the transport agency Main Roads deliberately downgraded their street signs in the hope of deterring potential thieves. As Main Roads representative Mick Edwards told *ABC News* in a 2015 interview, 'we're actually trying to make our signs on bridges look a little bit cheaper, so they sort of don't look as good ... if someone wants to steal them and hang them in their bar'. The transport agency achieved this 'less expensive' look by 'using old signage as the backing, and using a sticker over the top with the wording on it'. They hoped this 'cheapening' of Pilbara's street signs would curb the considerable cost and time spent replacing them.

From Canberra and Craigieburn to Tambo and Pilbara, public signs are mischief-making magnets. But no matter how cheap they look or how securely they're bolted on, I doubt public sign crime is ever going to STOP.

BIZARRE LAW #14

I love putting up 'do not disturb' signs at hotels. There's no better feeling than relaxing in a bubble bath and watching the latest season of *Below Deck Down Under*, safe in the knowledge that nobody is going to disturb your serenity. It would be great if you could put up 'do not disturb' signs everywhere you went. After all, life can be very disturbing.

South Australian legislators were on the right track when they drafted Section 50 of the *Summary Offences Act 1953* (SA), making it an offence to disturb 'another by wilfully pulling or ringing the doorbell of a house or by knocking at the door of a house' without a 'reasonable excuse'. The offence carries a maximum fine of $250.

Of course, what qualifies as a 'reasonable excuse' is up for interpretation. Nuisance knocks are obviously illegal, but what about religious missionaries or annoying neighbours or electricity company representatives? What is 'reasonable' for the knocker might be 'unreasonable' for the opener. According to *The Advertiser*, there were only 11 convictions of unlawfully ringing doorbells between May 1985 and June 2010, so you probably can't call the cops on any passerby who grinds your gears. South Australian introverts will have to continue to suffer in periodically interrupted silence.

BIZARRE LAW #15

S ection 47 of the *Summary Offences Act 1953* (SA) makes it an offence to kill, injure or take a homing pigeon 'without lawful authority'. According to the Act, a homing pigeon is defined as 'a pigeon having a ring affixed or attached to either or both legs'. It is also illegal to 'enter upon land for the purpose of killing, injuring, or taking any homing pigeon without lawful authority'. The law includes a provision that can get the defendant off the hook if 'the defendant was the owner or occupier of improved or cultivated land, or a person acting under the instructions of any such owner or occupier, and killed, injured or took the pigeon while it was actually upon that land or any building on that land'. The offence carries a maximum penalty of $250.

To modern readers, this law may seem a tad irrelevant. But it's important to remember that domesticated homing pigeons have been with us for thousands of years. I'm not going to write up a complete history of homing pigeons, but trust me when I say that people have been using pigeons to deliver messages for a very long time. The first 'official' regular pigeon mail service was set up in New Zealand in 1897. It was called the 'The Great Barrier

Pigeongram Agency'. According to the *Kashmir Observer*, 'each pigeon carried 5 messages and special Pigeon-Gram stamps were sold for each message carried'. (Pigeongram stamps are now collector's items and sell at auction for thousands of dollars.) The last pigeon mail service to close its doors was the Odisha Police Carrier Pigeon Service in Odisha, India. The service shut down in 2006 after 60 years in operation. The internet pushed 800 pigeons out of a job – I hope they found them alternative positions.

SA's homing pigeon protection law is obviously a relic of an age before WhatsApp, but who cares? I'm sure members of the South Australian Homing Pigeons Association are glad the legislation is still on the books. As far as I'm concerned, Section 47 should remain enshrined in law forever. Homing pigeons spent millennia delivering our mail. The least humans can do is protect them with a measly $250 fine. As loathe as I am to quote Mike Tyson, he was on the money when he tweeted: 'I don't understand why people would want to get rid of pigeons. They don't bother no one.'

SILLY SEASON

CHRISTMAS IS A TIME for giving. It's also a time for increased felony rates, financial stress and mental illness. They call it the 'silly season' for a reason, and it should come as no surprise that I found a Santa's sack worth of bizarre crime goodies for you to enjoy.

On 17 December 1933, Sydney's *The Sun* newspaper ran a story titled 'SANTA CLAUS WAS DRUNK IN STREET':

'Santa Claus' was arrested by the police last night.

They found him sitting on the doorway of a shop in Oxford-street, replete with long grey beard, red coat, top boots and all.

He could not stand up at their bidding, so he was taken to Darlinghurst Police Station and charged with drunkenness.

Let's hope St Nick got straightened out in time for Christmas Eve. Drunk driving rules apply even when your mode of transport is a flying sleigh.

Another 'Bad Santa' story was reported in *The Daily Mirror* on 8 February 1950 after 49-year-old military sergeant Vernon Daniels faced court in North Sydney on charges of insulting a police officer. The court was told that Vernon was dressed as Santa Claus on the day of the incident and entertaining children at a party in Bradfield Park. Police were called when Vernon kicked a 16-year-old boy who had crashed the party. (Vernon was a former amateur boxing champion known as the 'Human Hairpin', so I'm guessing a kick from Santa would have left a mark.) When Constable Maffasoinni questioned Vernon, he called the police officer a 'mug' and told him to 'go home and go to bed'. This is when Bradfield Park's resident Father Christmas was placed under arrest. Luckily for Vernon, Magistrate Thornton was full of good cheer. Although he found the case against Vernon proved, he still dismissed the charges, saying 'I believe that he is a man of excellent character, but on this occasion was annoyed by the boys and lost his temper'. It was Vernon's very own Christmas miracle.

But Christmas crimes don't always end happily, even when they're inspired by the spirit of the season. On Boxing Day 1951, 27-year-old Harold 'Dusty' Sheehan made the unconventional decision to break into Pentridge Prison in Melbourne. He was a former inmate and career criminal with a strong sense of Christmas giving. His plan was to infiltrate Pentridge under the cover of night, deliver gifts to his incarcerated comrades and break out the following evening. (Dusty Sheehan took 'ride or die' friendship to a whole new level.)

Dusty scaled the 20-foot-high bluestone prison wall at around 3.30am when he knew the northern watchtower would be unattended. According to *The Argus*, the real-life 'secret Santa' was carrying a suitcase containing '3lb tobacco, three bottles of whisky, a bottle of wine, some cigarettes, magazines, and newspapers'. (The ideal Christmas hamper when serving at Her Majesty's pleasure.) The prisoners were locked away for the night, so Dusty snuck into the reformatory mess hut and hid under a trapdoor in the floor. He waited there until 8.10am, when the prisoners were released from their cells. Two inmates retrieved the suitcase while Dusty remained hidden beneath the trapdoor. He planned to stay there until nightfall when he'd make his great escape. But things didn't go to plan and Dusty was busted by a prison warder at 11.35am. When the warder asked what he was doing, Dusty replied that he'd 'come in to help some—'. (The *Truth* blanked out the last word in the sentence, but I'm guessing it started with a 'c'.)

Dusty pleaded guilty to unlawful entry at his court hearing in Coburg. Judge Stafford sentenced him to six months in Pentridge for breaking into Pentridge (talk about a revolving prison door). It's sad to think such a heroic act of generosity was punished so harshly, but I take comfort in knowing that Dusty will always be remembered as the larrikin Santa who broke into prison to 'help some—'.

Sixty-five-year-old Brian [Redacted] learned the perils of playing Father Christmas on a trip to Bunnings in December 2022. Brian had played the role of Santa Claus at a charity event earlier in the day and was still in his resplendent red-and-white costume when he popped into a Bunnings in Frankson, Melbourne. According to Brian, he was innocently perusing the aisles and fellow customers were approaching him because of his outfit. According to the staff at Bunnings, Brian was behaving 'erratically' and refused to leave. Whatever the case, the cops were called to escort Brian from the premises. A scuffle ensued and Brian was doused in pepper spray. Footage of the incident shows him screaming in pain and police wrestling him to the ground. He was cuffed, then passed out and was taken to hospital. Bunnings later released a statement acknowledging the incident and thanking their team for managing the situation in a 'professional way'. Meanwhile, Brian told news outlets he'd be filing a complaint against police. I don't know what really happened and I couldn't find any follow-up reports. I just hope there weren't any children watching when Santa got maced. That sounds like a lifetime in therapy.

I have similar fears for the children who witnessed Darren [Redacted] assault an Easter bunny mascot in Albury, NSW, on 21 March 2013. The 46-year-old teacher violently tore the head off the mascot, who was entertaining a group of children at Bunnings. (It's important to clarify that I have nothing against Bunnings. It's not my fault two thematically related crimes went down at the same hardware chain.)

The Age described Darren as having 'stress related' problems, which may account for why he told the children: 'It's not the real Easter bunny. He's a fraud. Bunnings is a fraud taking down local hardware stores just like Mitre 10.' (Sounds like someone was working through some trauma unrelated to the Easter bunny.) This diatribe caused upset among the children (I can't imagine why) and a staff member asked Darren to leave. He refused to budge, so the staff member pushed against Darren's chest, causing him to tumble backwards ... onto a child.

On 16 July 2013, Darren appeared before Albury Local Court on charges of offensive behaviour, malicious damage and assault. Magistrate Tony Murray described Darren's behaviour as 'aggressive', 'totally unacceptable' and 'bizarre in the extreme'. Magistrate Murray adjourned the charges until December 2013 so Darren could undergo a 'treatment plan' for his mental health. This seems like a reasonable choice. If tearing the head off an Easter bunny mascot and lecturing small children on corporate competition isn't a sign of an emotional breakdown, I don't know what is.

The Easter bunny was on the other side of the law enforcement equation in April 2020 when he helped execute an arrest in the WA town of Collie. *ABC South West* reported that a police officer was patrolling the streets of Collie in an Easter bunny costume when he spotted a 35-year-old male wanted by law enforcement. A fellow officer called for back-up while the Easter bunny continued to monitor the criminal in question. According to the *ABC*, 'the man was on bail for several charges and has now been charged with breaching bail and obstructing the Easter bunny'. The report featured a photo of our righteous rabbit rocking a WA Police cap and giving two thumbs up to the camera. After the abuse he suffered in Albury, it was nice to see the Easter bunny take his power back.

THE ITALIAN WAITERS CLUB SIEGE

MARK 'CHOPPER' READ WAS the 'it' Aussie criminal of the 1990s and 2000s. The reformed crook was famous for his handlebar moustache, tall stories, strange charm and unique sense of humour. He rose to prominence off the back of his best-selling crime books, including *Chopper: From the Inside, Chopper 3: How to Shoot Friends & Influence People* and *Chopper 10½: The Popcorn Gangster.* His place in the zeitgeist was secured with the release of the 2000 hit film *Chopper*, with Eric Bana in the eponymous role. This gained Chopper an international following and a gig writing columns in *FHM* magazine. Chopper remained in the public eye until his death in 2013. As journalist Garth Cartwright said of the iconic ex-con: 'Not since Ned Kelly has an Australian criminal enjoyed such public adulation.'

Before becoming a writer and media personality, Chopper was a street thug, gang leader and standover man. Between the ages of 20 and 38, he spent no more than 13 months out of prison. His rap sheet included convictions for armed robbery, arson, assault and attempted murder. His longest sentence was for the attempted abduction of County Court Judge Bill Martin, which landed him behind bars for 13 years. It was a big sentence for a big screw-up.

The ill-fated scheme began when Chopper befriended armed robber

Jimmy Loughnan during his first stint in Pentridge Prison. Upon his release in 1977, Chopper promised Jimmy he'd find a way to free him before his sentence was up (Jimmy still had another six years to serve). Never one to back down from a challenge, Chopper hatched a plan to kidnap a local magistrate and use him as collateral to negotiate Loughnan's release.

On Australia Day 1978, he headed down to the County Court in Melbourne CBD with a sawn-off shotgun hidden in his trench coat. According to an interview with *The Age*, Chopper 'marched in, climbed on the judge's bench, put the gun to his forehead, and demanded Jimmy's release'. Judge Bill Martin's chief of staff leapt into action, secured the gun and wrestled Chopper to the ground. (According to some accounts, Judge Martin kicked Chopper in the balls, which I hope is true.) Chopper was arrested, charged and sent back to Pentridge, where Loughnan stabbed him in a premeditated attack (talk about ungrateful!).

During his first stint in Pentridge, Chopper had founded the infamous 'Overcoat Gang', a group dedicated to scams, extortions, protection rackets and heinous acts of violence. One of the gang members was Amos Atkinson. He loved Chopper and wanted to be like Chopper. So it was only natural that Atkinson would try to get Chopper out of prison in the same way Chopper tried to get Loughnan out of prison (it's the circle of life).

A month after the County Court kidnapping caper, 19-year-old Atkinson and his friend Robert Williams laid siege to an Italian restaurant in the Melbourne CBD, took 30 people hostage and demanded Chopper's release. The restaurant in question was the Italian Waiters Club, a late-night dining spot for the city's powerful, influential and well-connected. Among the diners that evening was the manager of the Princes Theatre, Roger Meyers, who described the events as follows:

We'd finished our meal and were having a quiet chat when two men ran up the stairs brandishing sawn-off shotguns. One of them shot into the door frame, but after that it became a waiting game. They pushed me to the floor behind the serving area, and poured wine and bolognaise sauce all over me. Both men were upset and angry, and had no idea how to get out of the situation.

If you're getting the vibe that Atkinson and Williams were in over their heads, you'd be correct. Atkinson began by sending out a hostage to tell the police if Chopper wasn't released in the next 24 hours he would start killing people. This didn't get him very far, so he sent out another hostage to make a second demand: could the police please bring his mother to the restaurant?

Mrs Atkinson arrived at the Italian Waiters Club in her pyjamas and dressing gown. (I'm guessing it was well past her bedtime.) The story goes that she walked into the restaurant, whacked her son on the head with her handbag and told him to stop this foolishness – or words to that effect. Amos was suitably cowed and surrendered to the police as the sun rose.

Atkinson was sentenced to five years in prison. But it wasn't a total bust. At least he was back inside with his hero Chopper.

He remained a dedicated fanboy and continued to emulate his idol. After Chopper voluntarily had his ears cut off to avoid a lethal prison attack, Atkinson followed suit and got his ears cut off as well. And you thought Collingwood fans were obsessive!

As for Mrs Atkinson, her story is lost to history. I like to think Victoria Police offered her a gig as a hostage negotiator. After all, what would be more terrifying to a hardened criminal than a sleep-deprived mum with a handbag?

VERSACE NECKLACE FISHING ROD THEFT

EARLY IN THE MORNING of 24 February 2020, a man in a blue windcheater and tracksuit pants (comfort is key) robbed a high-end boutique on Little Collins Street in Melbourne CBD. The thief used a fishing rod to hook an item of jewellery from a mannequin in the front window. CCTV footage showed the man making a hole in the window and inserting the rod through to access the display. He must have been accustomed to the slow pace of fishing because he spent over three hours securing his catch.

The boutique's owner, Steven Adigrati, was stunned by the theft. 'I couldn't believe it,' he told *Nine News*. 'Three-and-a-half hours ... trying to get this necklace, was amazing. Hook, line, and sinker.'

Detective Senior Constable Bede Whitty shared Adigrati's surprise. He described the crime as 'blatant and bold', telling *ABC News* that he had 'not seen someone use a fishing rod to commit a burglary in the past'. (I doubt theft by fishing rod is a terribly common occurrence outside of Bugs Bunny cartoons.)

But the blatant and bold burglar might have been disappointed when he tried to palm off his hard-won prize. The stolen item was a golden necklace bearing the iconic Versace Medusa head. It *looked* expensive, but it wasn't expensive, at least not by designer jewellery standards. The necklace was a show piece priced at $799, which doesn't add up to the best hourly rate for an industrious thief working the night shift.

As they like to say in fishing circles: 'There is a reason they call it fishing and not catching.'

INSTANT KARMA

ACCORDING TO THE BUDDHIST doctrine of karma, we cannot escape the consequences of our actions. If we do bad things, we will experience bad outcomes. It is an inescapable law of the universe.

Cut to Brisbane, 29 December 2022. Pool technician David Brain was working a job when he noticed a man trying to break into his ute. David chased the robber (let's call him 'Dwayne') who dashed back to his motorbike where his female companion (let's call her 'Tiffany') was waiting. David grabbed the front of the motorbike and confronted the pair.

'I tried to wrangle them off the bike,' David told *Nine News*, 'but that didn't work, so I grabbed my phone. I thought I better get a good picture of his face.'

Dwayne and Tiffany were wearing bike helmets (safety first), but David still managed to capture footage of their faces. There was a brief confrontation before the dynamic duo broke free of David's grip and drove off.

But they didn't get far. '[Dwayne] wasn't very good at taking off,' said David. 'Next minute I know ... he hit the pole and came unstuck.'

Tiffany flew off the bike and let out a scream. David recorded her climbing back onto the bike minus most of her left thumb. 'Check your wife!' David shouted at Dwayne. 'Look after her! You want a first-aid kit?'

But Dwayne didn't take David up on his generous offer. He sped away with Tiffany bleeding on the back of the bike. They drove for about 25 minutes before Dwayne dumped Tiffany at the side of the Logan Motorway (what a guy). She flagged down a passing ambulance, presumably with her right hand, and Dwayne drove off into the sunset.

David attributed Tiffany's missing thumb to 'karma'. 'Lucky I didn't do anything myself,' he said. 'They done it to themselves.' It's a morality tale worthy of the Buddhist sutras.

The harsh hand of karma was also at work when a 41-year-old Queensland man (let's call him 'Harold') stole two motorbikes from a store in West Ipswich on the morning of 15 October 2021. Harold used a yellow front-end loader to smash into the store and collect the motorbikes in the loader's front bucket (giving new meaning to the term 'shoplifting'). The police were quick to arrive at the scene, so Harold ditched the motorbikes and made a lumbering getaway.

A front-end loader isn't the ideal mode of transport for a police chase, so Harold detoured onto a railway corridor to avoid the cops. He drove along the tracks, got off the tracks and got onto another set of tracks. The loader crashed through yards and fences, knocked out railway signals and caused general destruction. But karma came along and brought Harold's heavy-duty joy ride to an end. The loader slid into a tree and got stuck near Dinmore railway station. Harold was found by the police dog squad unit hiding in a creek shortly afterwards (so glamorous). He was charged with multiple offences, including wilful damage and dangerous operation of a motor vehicle. As I once read on a bumper sticker, 'People who create their own drama deserve their own karma.'

But my favourite case of karma clapback comes from a failed assassination attempt carried out in Greenacre, Sydney on 7 February 2022. In the wee hours of the morning, an unnamed assassin (let's call him 'Bill') fired multiple shots into the home of 24-year-old Haysam [Redacted], who was on a $1 million bail for an alleged kidnapping attempt. Thankfully, Haysam wasn't injured.

Bill sped away in his white Commodore (the classic car for assassins everywhere) and parked in a nearby street. Video footage shows him trying to destroy the evidence by setting fire to the car. But this backfired (literally) when he accidentally set fire to himself. He was recorded running away from the Commodore with the left arm of his hoodie ablaze. (The footage looks like a low-rent version of *Ghost Rider*.) *The Daily Mail* called it a case of 'instant karma'. You might also call it 'stupidity', but 'karma' has a nicer ring.

MAKE YOURSELF AT HOME

A N UNUSUAL BURGLARY WAS perpetrated in south-west Melbourne
on 4 January 2019. Security cameras caught footage of a man in his
30s breaking into the Laverton residence of 55-year-old truck driver
Steven Freeman. After receiving a warm welcome from Mr Freeman's
affable German shepherd Jesse, the unknown man (let's call him 'Jeremy')
made himself right at home. Rather than doing typical 'burglar things'
such as ransacking drawers or upturning furniture, Jeremy headed to the
kitchen for a snack.

'He ate all my Cadbury Favourites,' Mr Freeman told *Nine News*.
'There were several cans of drink which he demolished ... he probably
would have cooked himself dinner if I didn't come home.'

Once Jeremy was done raiding the chocolate stash, he did a load of
washing (his own, not Steven's) and trimmed his toenails (gross). He was
about to jump in the shower when Mr Freeman arrived home. Jeremy
made a quick exit, stealing a set of speakers on his way out. On the
upside, Jeremy left the Turkish delights untouched, which I'm sure Mr
Freeman appreciated.

Jeremy's casual approach to burglary reminded me of another case
I read in *The Henty Observer and Culcairn Shire Register* (I do my
research!). On 19 November 1937, the newspaper ran a report headlined

'STRANGE ARREST. ALLEGED BURGLAR GOT DRUNK. SUCCUMBED TO DECANTER OF WHISKY':

A highly unusual arrest which had all the elements of pure farce took place in Hill Street, Orange, when police entered a house and found an alleged burglar drunk on the premises. From their investigations the police officers discovered that clothing and other goods had been neatly packed into suitcases ready for removal.

The man arrested had apparently imbibed not wisely, but rather too well from a decanter of whisky in the house and he offered no resistance when the police arrested him.

It is stated that entry was gained to the house through a window, which had been reached by jumping from the top of a tank. A pair of man's boots were found on top of the tank.

The occupants of the house were absent at the time and someone nearby, knowing that they were away from Orange, became suspicious when a light was noticed in a room. – As there is quite a number of alleged burglaries taking place locally, why not try having a spot of whisky handy?

Maybe it's a good idea to leave chocolates and brown liquor out for burglars (like the 'home invaders' version of milk and cookies for Santa). You're probably not going to score any presents, but if you're very lucky, they might leave you a pile of toenails to clean up.

FORTUNE TOLD AND TAKEN

Australians who love their daily horoscope or calling the psychic hotline may be shocked to learn that fortune-telling was illegal for most of Australia's colonial history. The states and territories only began removing the ban in the 21st century. In fact, there are still prohibitions on the books in the NT and SA.

It's worth flagging that the ban was never widely enforced and lots of people still practised fortune-telling. It wasn't illegal to set up a fortune-telling business or advertise yourself as a fortune-teller. It was just illegal to *receive money* for fortune-telling. This offence was usually time-consuming to prove, so most of the time the cops didn't bother. (They probably had better things to do, such as tracking down night soil men who left shit in the streets or busting the shoplifters at Cole's Book Arcade.)

I should also clarify that the NT and SA laws don't prohibit fortune-telling *per se*; they just ban fortune-telling *with intent to deceive*. Darwin residents can cast the runes all day long without fear of a SWAT team breaking down the door.

Law enforcement has always been more interested in fortune-tellers when they use their profession to commit other crimes (such as stealing money). There were a few fortune-telling scams doing the rounds in early 20th-century Australia. These usually involved a colourfully dressed woman, an easily duped man and a handful of cash. Here are four great examples of 'psychics' who were more interested in taking fortunes than telling them:

UNFORTUNATE FORTUNE 1

On 27 June 1914, *The Age* told the story of a 'scenic artist' named Eric Jamieson who was visiting a shop in Albert Park, Melbourne when he met a 'young woman of attractive appearance' who offered to tell his fortune. He agreed 'just for the sport of it' and 'she prophesised a magnificent future for him, mapping out a wonderful business career, and telling him of domestic prospects'. She said she couldn't go any further with her predictions 'until he placed all the gold he had with him in his right hand' (an oddly specific request). Jamieson was anxious to know all the good things coming his way, so he grabbed his gold and held it in his hand:

> The attractive girl caught hold of his hand, waved her other hand in the impressive way of the romancer, told him more of the future, and then, gently doubling up his fingers upon his gold, went out. Then he counted his money two minutes later – a sovereign and a half sovereign were missing.

Police tracked down 22-year-old Georgina Neate, who was charged with larceny and granted bail. As for our victim, I couldn't find any evidence of an artist named Eric Jamieson whose career took off, so it looks like Georgina was talking crap.

UNFORTUNATE FORTUNE 2

On 2 June 1926, *The Telegraph* reported the case of a Melbourne doctor who found himself a few pounds short after a run-in with a 30-year-old fortune-teller named Olga Adams. Adams was described as a 'plump woman' who was 'dressed in characteristic Eastern (European) dress of many colours, with strings of pink and gold beads round her neck, and many rings on her fingers'. She also had a tattoo on her left hand, which was a bold look for 1926. (The report doesn't mention what it was a tattoo of, but I'm guessing it was something tasteful, such as a skull and crossbones.)

Adams brought 'her little boy' to see Dr Thomas Willis at his clinic in Malvern to treat a wound on his finger. After Dr Willis was done fixing him up, Adams offered to tell his fortune. Willis was sceptical and declined her offer. But she wasn't taking 'no' for an answer:

> He told her to go on, but to cut it short. She then said, 'Put some silver coins in your hand.' He did so and she spoke 'a lot of rot about good luck and good times'. She then asked for paper money. He got £3 10s from a drawer. She went on talking about all the money he would receive.
>
> 'She asked for a towel,' continued Dr. Willis. 'I got one and she told me to tie the notes in the end of it. I did so and she then seized the towel by the end that did not have the notes in, and gave it three sharp flicks, striking the table and saying, 'Your bad luck has gone now.'
>
> 'When I untied the towel the notes had gone. I asked her for them and she said, "You will find them on the table in the morning". I thought that I would and never worried over them at the moment. I thought she was only showing me one of her tricks. The whole thing was a remarkable piece of legerdemain.'

In case you were wondering, 'legerdemain' is an old-timey word for 'sleight of hand'.

After the money failed to magically appear on Dr Willis's desk, he called the cops and Adams was charged with larceny. Her lawyer pushed the responsibility back on Dr Willis, arguing if he had 'used a little common sense and insisted on the return of the money there would not have been any trouble'. (Talk about victim-blaming!) The magistrate disagreed and the fortune-teller was fined £10 (equivalent to A$975).

UNFORTUNATE FORTUNE 3

On 17 January 1935, *The Courier-Mail* ran a piece titled 'Fortune Told and Taken'. It reported the case of a Brisbane man named Leslie Henderson, who was busy delivering ice cream when he stopped at a shop in North Pine. Here he met a 21-year-old woman named Marjorie Stevens, who the *Truth* newspaper described as 'tall and dark, attired in a long, wide skirt, bangles dangling on her arms'. The fabulously dressed Marjorie offered to tell Henderson's fortune. He happily agreed. According to *The Courier-Mail*:

> She asked what was in the bag he was carrying by a strap round his shoulder. He said it contained £37 in notes, money belonging to his firm. The woman asked to be allowed to look at it, as that would assist her in her prophecy. Henderson handed some of the money to her. She held it in her hand while she made signs above it, in the course of her 'fortune-telling.' Later she left the shop and drove off in a car ... Henderson then discovered that she had taken the sum of £17/10 with her.

Marjorie was fined £2 and ordered to pay restitution of £17 (the equivalent of A$2250). I just hope Henderson's ice cream didn't melt while the drama was going down.

UNFORTUNATE FORTUNE 4

On 22 May 1946, police warned readers of *The Argus* against an all-too-familiar fortune-telling deception:

> Following complaints received yesterday, police issued a warning against a ... fortune-teller who has been operating in the Victoria Market, and who has been allegedly using her 'trade' to aid in thefts. Her modus operandi, police say, was to offer to 'bless' her 'clients' money, and, by sleight of hand, extract one or two pound notes from his 'roll.' Fortunately for a man who reported the matter, the [fortune-teller's] sleight of hand was not as effective as she had apparently hoped, as he saw the edge of a pound showing from her hand. When he forced her fingers apart he found two other notes which had been extracted from his money.

Busted! She didn't see that coming.

Cases of fortune-telling fraud continued to be prosecuted in Australia until the 1980s. According to solicitor Nicola Bowes, there was a case prosecuted in 1986 of a fortune-teller who convinced her clients to give over almost $400,000 worth of possessions and cash that she claimed were 'haunted'. (I hate it when I withdraw a $50 note that's possessed by the ghost of a 19th-century fishmonger. That's why I prefer tap-and-go.) She promised to return the valuables once she'd 'cleansed' them. But she didn't, because she was lying. The unfortunate fortune-teller was sent to prison.

I looked for proof that one of these criminal clairvoyants had broken out of jail so I could use my favourite fortune-telling joke. My search proved unsuccessful, but here's the joke anyway: 'What do you call a short fortune-teller who just escaped from prison? A short medium at large.'

MINION MADNESS

IN 2017, AN UNNAMED person dressed as a Minion from *Despicable Me* stole a 20-centimetre circle of grass from a front lawn in Kalgoorlie, WA. (I was tempted to leave that sentence as a standalone statement, but because I'm nice, I'll fill in the rest of the details.)

Brad Nicklin was nursing a hangover on a Sunday morning when he noticed a missing patch in his carefully manicured lawn. He inspected the damage and determined it was a deliberate act of sabotage. Brad had recently boasted on Snapchat how well his lawn was doing, so he suspected one of his friends was trying to teach him a lesson. (You can always rely on Aussie mates to smack you down if you're starting to feel good about yourself.)

He checked his security camera footage and watched as a bright yellow, one-eyed, adult-sized Minion shovelled up a circle of lawn. 'We couldn't stop laughing,' Brad told *WA today*. 'All in good fun, but my beautiful lawn!'

The culprit also created a Facebook page called 'Carl Minion', which showcased photos of the costumed thief fleeing the scene of the crime, as well as a video of 'Carl' watering the stolen patch of grass.

But the identity of the lawn larcenist remained elusive. *Mashable* contacted Carl, but he declined to comment. As far as I know, the rascally Minion is still at large, bringing proud lawn owners to their knees with a shovel and a toothy cartoon smile.

FOR THE EXPOSURE

On 11 March 1992, two French street performers were arrested at the Adelaide Festival of Arts. The performers were part of a group called 'Ilotopie', which the festival program described as a 'bizarre French urban art troupe'. The performers were making their debut Adelaide public performance when the police rudely interrupted. The cops apparently didn't appreciate a group of French people wearing nothing more than G-strings and body paint moving their bodies in interesting ways in front of the South Australian Museum.

It looks like things got messy when police tried to arrest 37-year-old performer Raymond Blard, who was charged with 'hindering police, resisting arrest and property damage'. The 'damaged property' in question was a police uniform that got covered in green body paint (which is what happens when you stop a French performance artist from expressing himself).

The other arrestee was 24-year-old Myriam Prijent. She was wearing a G-string, covered in red body paint and charged with 'offensive behaviour'.

The Canberra Times noted that Ilotopie had performed 'without incident' in other Australian cities and around the world. Evidently, bright red European boobs were too much for early 90s Adelaide law enforcement to bear.

Another scantily clad performer was arrested in Adelaide in 2021. But this time the problem wasn't so much the lack of clothes as the lack of decorum.

A 32-year-old musician and former porn star (let's call him 'Jim') became known as the 'underwear rocker' after he began holding regular Sunday afternoon performances in front of his Salisbury Downs garage wearing nothing but sneakers and underwear. A concert would typically last 45 minutes and featured Jim rocking out on his electric guitar to a set of self-written songs.

'I'm only ever greeted by smiles,' he told *ABC News*. 'We have a really sort of good thing going down here.'

Jim said that some of his neighbours had even donated instruments to support his creative efforts. But not everyone was supportive. There were complaints about the noise and colourful lyrics.

'I don't have a problem with him playing,' one neighbour told *Radio Adelaide*, 'but what I do have a problem with is the F- and C-bombs he continually drops ... he should be booked for indecent language.'

Police responded to these complaints on 13 June 2021 and arrested Jim mid-performance for failure to comply with an environmental protection order. He compared the arrest to the epic battle of good and evil in the original *Star Wars* trilogy: 'It was like being Luke Skywalker and people from the Death Star told me I wouldn't play my guitar anymore,' he told *news.com.au*. 'That's not right. That goes against my freedoms.'

In answer to the residents who made complaints, he said: 'If people think playing guitar and singing is a crime, then pish-posh. Get bent.'

Jim was ordered to appear in court on 17 August 2021. He arrived dressed in brown cowboy boots, black pants, a brightly patterned shirt, a Sgt Pepper's Lonely Hearts Club Band–style jacket, a yellow beaded necklace and round-rimmed glasses with orange lenses.

'My lawyers have told me that I'm awesome,' he told *Seven News*. (It's always good to have encouraging legal counsel.)

But Jim couldn't make his court appearance because he refused to wear a COVID mask (it was one item of clothing too many). Luckily for him, his failure to comply with COVID restrictions didn't stop his lawyer from getting the charges dropped on the grounds of 'mental impairment'.

Jim was back in the news in 2023 after he made an application to the South Australian Civil and Administrative Tribunal to have his firearms licence reinstated. According to *The Advertiser*, Jim's licence had been cancelled in the wake of his 2021 arrest, when police seized an 'unknown number' of firearms from his home and raised concerns over his 'bizarre' behaviour.

Jim's brother spoke in support of the 'underwear rocker' at the tribunal hearing, saying his brother 'contributed significantly to the community through his music'. Jim also submitted a psychological report confirming he was mentally fit to bear arms. But the tribunal ruled against him, saying Jim couldn't be 'mentally impaired' in one case and 'mentally un-impaired' in another. (The tribunal used different language, but that's basically what they meant.) He would have to live without his guns.

At least the tribunal couldn't revoke Jim's sweet style or the spirit of rock 'n' roll. In the eternal words of the late, great singer Larry Williams: 'Rock and roll has no beginning and no end for it is the very pulse of life itself.'

Rock on, Jim. Rock on.

SERVO SCREW-UPS

THE FOLLOWING STORIES ARE tied together by two common themes: service stations and stupidity. They paint a picture of petrol-scented absurdity so profound that I wonder if there's any sense to the universe at all.

SERVO SCREW-UP 1

On 9 May 2005, a man disguised in a scarf, beanie and sun visor walked into a service station in Bundaberg, Queensland and casually handed a note to the attendant. The note claimed the man was carrying a weapon and demanded the attendant hand over cash. But he wasn't carrying a weapon – he was carrying a skateboard. The attendant was suitably unimpressed and told the would-be-robber to 'bugger off' – or words to that effect. The thief must have taken this rejection to heart because he left the servo right away. The service station manager said the staff were 'okay' after their run-in with the note-and-skateboard-wielding bandit.

SERVO SCREW-UP 2

On 2 July 2012, 22-year-old Tonee [Redacted] robbed a service station in Arundel on the Gold Coast. She was carrying a flick knife and sporting a low-cut top, which earned her the nickname 'the buxom bandit' after footage of the robbery (and her cleavage) caught the attention of international media. Her getaway driver told police that 'the buxom bandit' had deliberately lowered her top beforehand, telling friends she wanted to give the service station attendant 'something to look at'. She certainly gave the police something to look at on the CCTV cameras when she failed to wear a mask or any kind of disguise. She also left fingerprints at the crime scene because she only wore a glove on her right hand. (Someone should have mentioned that the left hand also leaves fingerprints.) After five days on the run, she was in police custody. Tonee was sentenced to four years in prison, where the outfits are decidedly less flattering.

SERVO SCREW-UP 3

In September 2013, 19-year-old Kristian [Redacted] robbed a service station in Mount Barker, South Australia, with the help of two underage accomplices. He threatened the attendant with a knife and made off with a stash of cigarettes and cash.

Kristian was caught and arrested soon after. He appeared before Adelaide Magistrate's Court in April 2014, where he pled guilty to a charge of aggravated assault. He confessed to consuming 'copious amounts of alcohol' before the theft. He also claimed to be under another pernicious influence – the video game *Grand Theft Auto*.

'It was submitted that, in your alcoholic stupor, you tried to emulate or replicate the [video] game in real life and rob the service station,' said Judge Paul Rice. 'That game is a well-known and well-used game and this is the first time I've heard it said that it may have been the basis upon or the reason for which an offender then went on to rob a service station.'

Needless to say, the '*Grand Theft Auto* made me do it' defence failed to convince Judge Rice, who sentenced Kristian to four years and 11 months in prison. Game over.

SERVO SCREW-UP 4

In May 2015, Queensland Police Service released footage of a bungled ATM heist at a service station in Townsville. The video was titled 'Attempted ATM theft, Townsville' and dubbed with music to heighten its comedic effect.

The thief (let's call him 'Joe') is shown pulling up in a white ute and smashing through the store's glass front doors with a paving slab and a sledgehammer. Joe crawls into the store and ties a chain to the ATM. During the heist, he fails to notice the chain has uncoupled and is no longer attached to the vehicle. He drives away, leaving the chain and the ATM behind (believe me, it's quality viewing).

The video shows Joe returning to the servo for a second go. He attempts to reconnect the chain but hasn't parked close enough for it to reach the ute. He pulls on the chain a couple of times before giving up and driving off empty-handed. I don't know why he didn't at least try to reposition the ute. Then again, I don't claim to understand the inner workings of such a singular mind.

Joe's loss turned into a massive gain for the Queensland Police Service's YouTube account. Within a few days of release, the video had reached over 500,000 views. At the time of writing, this number had tripled. If you're ever feeling bad about yourself or your life choices, I highly recommend you check it out.

SERVO SCREW-UP 5

On 19 March 2018, a man in a grey hoodie robbed a service station in Ascot, Perth. Before committing the crime, he walked up to the front door of the service station and took a moment to work out how to hide his face. He experimented with a sunglasses and hoodie combo but ultimately opted for a balaclava, which he donned in full view of the servo's CCTV camera. He robbed the store, unaware that his face would soon appear on the *Today* show with the caption: 'Perth's Dumbest Crim'.

SERVO SCREW-UP 6

On April 2019, a man held up a service station in Caboolture, Queensland wearing a 'Plus Fitness' reusable shopping bag on his head as a disguise. He threatened the service station attendant with a knife and demanded she open the cash register. He took the money from the till and ordered the attendant to hand over several packets of cigarettes. He then removed the bag from his head and used it to stash away his loot, giving the CCTV cameras a perfect view of his face. Someone should have told him that you can't use a bag to hide your face *and* carry your loot the same time. It doesn't work.

SERVO SCREW-UP 7

On 26 January 2022, 19-year-old Lachlan [Redacted] attempted to hold up a service station in Woodville North, Adelaide. According to *The Advertiser*, Lachlan was under the influence of several illicit and prescription drugs at the time, which may explain why the service station attendant 'thought it was a joke' when he demanded cash from the till. He demanded several more times, but the attendant continued to say 'no'. To be taken more seriously, Lachlan thrust a knife in the attendant's direction but was hampered by the COVID-safe screen, which stopped the knife from making contact with the bemused attendant. Frustrated by failure, he started smashing things up in the store.

Lachlan appeared before Adelaide District Court in April 2022, where the prosecutor described the crime as 'brazen' and 'stupid'. Lachlan received a two-year suspended sentence but was back in trouble later that year when police busted him with 47 MDMA (ecstasy) tablets stashed down the front of his pants. At first, he said he didn't know where the drugs came from. (Don't you hate it when a stash of MDMA magically appears in your pants?) Then he claimed the drugs were for 'personal use' and that he took around ten tablets a day! Nobody believed this (because it's insane) and he admitted to being a drug dealer. Lachlan was sentenced to four years and nine months in jail with a non-parole period of two years and eight months. Some people aren't cut out for a life of crime.

SERVO SCREW-UP 8

On 15 April 2021, a young man (let's call him 'Richard') robbed a service station in Forestville, Sydney. He wielded a ten-centimetre knife and demanded the attendant put 'all the money' in the Coles bag he'd brought with him. He left with $397.50.

A month later, Richard robbed the same service station. He wielded a 20 centimetre knife and demanded the attendant put 'all the money' in the Coles bag he'd brought with him. He left with $188.50.

A few days later, Richard drove to the same service station to buy a pie and chocolate milk. The attendant on duty was the same one he'd robbed a few days earlier. The attendant recognised Richard (it's amazing how well you remember someone after they've held you up at knifepoint), wrote down his licence plate number and called the cops. Richard was arrested and charged.

I'm glad to say this story ends on a somewhat uplifting note. Between his arrest and court appearance, Richard worked hard to turn his life around. He underwent treatment for his crystal meth addiction, got a full-time job and pursued an apprenticeship. Judge Christopher Robison described him as a 'model example of how one can change'. Richard was found guilty of armed robbery but permitted to serve his prison sentence 'in the community' under the supervision of community correction (provided he stuck to the rules). He was ordered to continue his drug rehabilitation and serve 300 hours of community service. The sentence was based on Judge Robison's ruling that Richard was 'extremely unlikely to reoffend' because of all the good work he'd done on himself.

It just goes to show that when people try to do better, there is some sense in the universe. Not much, but enough to make you smile.

BIZARRE LAW #16

The opening credit sequence of *Sex and the City* features the mysteriously affluent newspaper columnist Carrie Bradshaw walking the streets of Manhattan. She's having a fabulous time until her outfit (a pink tank top with an oyster-white three-tier tutu skirt and matching satin waistband) gets splashed by a passing bus driving through a puddle. Carrie's smile turns to a frown as her tutu is touched by tragedy.

Admittedly, Carrie Bradshaw isn't the world's most sympathetic character. (The words 'self-absorbed', 'immature' and 'deceitful' spring to mind.) But you can understand why she feels upset when the bus splashes water on her tutu. If you've ever been splashed by a passing vehicle, you'll know how it can dampen your day. I'm sure a lot of NSW pedestrians were supportive of regulation 291–3 in *Road Rules NSW 2014*, which made it an offence for passing motorists to splash mud on passengers waiting at bus stops. The regulation required drivers to 'take due care, by slowing or stopping' their vehicle, to avoid splashing mud on:

(a) any person in or on a bus, or

(b) any person entering or leaving any stationary bus, or

(c) any person waiting at any bus stop,

if the bus concerned is being used to provide a public passenger service or the bus stop concerned is a stop relating to buses used for that purpose.

I have some questions. Why would someone 'in or on' a bus need protection from splashing mud? What is the difference between 'in' or 'on' a bus? When they say 'on' a bus, do they mean someone literally standing *on top* of a bus, like Guy Pearce in *The Adventures of Priscilla, Queen of the Desert*? Why specifically prohibit splashing 'mud'? What about 'water' or 'muddy water'? At what point does a puddle turn from water to mud? What happens if you try to take 'due care' but end up splashing mud because the whole road is covered in mud? Do you have to pull over until the bus empties or the mud dries up? In their rush to protect the citizens of NSW, lawmakers may have failed to think through the complexities that surround a drive-by splashing.

The maximum penalty for breaching regulation 291–3 was a fine of $2200. In most instances, errant drivers would receive an on-the-spot fine of $187 (because escalating a mud-splashing incident to court is a lot of paperwork).

In an interview in 2015, University of Technology Sydney Law Professor Anita Stuhmcke described the regulation as 'a sensible piece of legislation ... [that is reflective of] goodness, love, civil society, politeness, consideration for others [and] respect for bus stops and clothing'. She described herself as 'a devotee of the message sent by this regulatory framework around bus stops, mud and indifferent motorists'. She promised to 'always and only arrange to meet colleagues, friends and even strangers on rainy days at bus stops'.

Sadly for Professor Stuhmcke, the legislation was repealed in 2020. Even though pedestrians are still protected under the state's negligent driving laws, there are no longer any rules specifically relating to bus stop mud splashes. But perhaps that's for the best. It reminds me of something Carrie Bradshaw said about Mr Big that also applies to regulation 291–3: 'It's a good idea in theory, but somehow it doesn't quite work.'

STOLEN SPECIMENS

ON 21 MAY 1947, 38-year-old Englishman Colin Wyatt was fined £100 at West Ham's Court London for stealing over 1500 butterfly specimens from Australian museums and collections.

The Sydney Morning Herald reported that Wyatt was a 'learned entomologist' who spoke several languages, including Norwegian. He was also an accomplished landscape painter and skier who had 'won the English ski-jumping championship at St. Mortiz, Switzerland, in 1936'. (Wyatt was quite the Renaissance man!)

Wyatt arrived in Australia in 1939, where he hosted two exhibitions of his paintings and stole butterflies from collections around the country. He had a taste for rare specimens and took 'more than 120 of the beautiful metallic blue butterflies of the genus *Ogyris*, which are the cream of the great Waterhouse Collection in the Sydney Museum'. He stole butterflies from the Melbourne Museum while the 'keeper of butterflies', Mr AN Burns, was away on a 'butterfly hunting excursion' in NSW. (It never pays to leave your station when you're the keeper of the butterflies.) Wyatt used his 'credentials as an entomologist, and his engaging manner' to access the museum's butterfly cabinets and steal 827 specimens. He also stole 'a large, brilliant butterfly' from the Brisbane Museum and several specimens from the Council for Scientific and Industrial Research in Canberra (which was renamed 'CSIRO' in 1949.)

His most mysterious heist was the theft of 603 specimens from the Adelaide Museum. The museum staff had no idea how he had accessed the butterfly cases. They speculated that 'he hid in the building and was locked in for the night'. (I'm assuming he pulled off the heist in a Batman villain–style butterfly costume and left behind a leopard moth caterpillar as a calling card.)

Shortly after his return to England in January 1947, police visited Wyatt's home in Farnham, Surrey, where they found cases containing over 3000 butterfly specimens. Entomologists from the British Museum 'identified most of them as the ones missing from Australia'. The stolen specimens 'were carefully packed by British Museum experts and shipped to Adelaide'. The experts tasked with sorting through the specimens were none too pleased with Wyatt for screwing up their filing system. He had thrown 'into confusion the accurate classification which had been made by Australian scientists over several decades'. It was an epic entomology fail.

As for Wyatt, a hefty fine, public disgrace and several pissed-off experts weren't enough to stop him from pursuing his passion. He continued to travel the world like the entomology equivalent of James Bond, collecting butterflies everywhere he went. He even wrote an autobiography titled *Going Wild: The Autobiography of a Bug Hunter* (which conveniently fails to mention his criminal activities Down Under). He died in a plane crash in Guatemala in 1975, leaving behind a collection of approximately 90,000 specimens. (We can also only wonder what his home decor must have been like. Housing 90,000 entomological specimens is quite the interior design challenge!)

On 12 March 2003, officers for the Independent Commission Against Corruption (ICAC) searched the residence of 53-year-old Hank [Redacted] in Londonderry, Sydney. According to ICAC, the search 'revealed in all corners of his house and an outside shed and several large freezers, thousands of zoological specimens, including skulls, skeletons, skins and complete animal specimens in alcohol'. Hank's home was a treasure trove of natural history wonders, including a rare Tasmanian tiger skull and a taxidermy lion valued at $50,000. It's estimated the total collection was worth more than $1 million.

Rewind to December 1996, when Hank secured a job as a pest controller at Sydney's Australian Museum. This was a dream come true for the natural history buff, who had been collecting zoological specimens for many years. 'Before I was 20 I had already collected chimpanzee skeletons, leopard skeletons [and] monkeys,' he told *SBS News*.

But his enthusiasm turned to dismay when he saw how some of the specimens were being stored. According to Hank, 'there were things lying around the place' in a state of disrepair. 'You can't store stuffed animals in a building that's full of pigeons,' he said. 'It's like there was no interest.'

We have no way of knowing how significant (or genuine) the problem really was. I'm inclined to take Hank's account with the tiniest grain of salt because he used this apparent 'neglect' as justification for stealing hundreds of items from the museum between 1997 and 2002. 'It became an obsession,' Hank told ICAC investigators. 'I just collected 'em ... It is just something I can't explain.'

As the museum's pest controller, he enjoyed wide-ranging access to the collection, with very little oversight. This gave him the opportunity to steal with impunity – which he did.

It didn't take long for museum staff to realise things were going missing. Hank was the primary suspect, but the museum couldn't act without proof. The police were summoned in 1998 but failed to find any evidence of Hank's guilt (they obviously didn't search his home!). The museum increased its security, but the thefts continued. In late 1999, Hank was transferred to the palaeontology division of the museum. This restricted his access to the collection but didn't stop him from pilfering whenever possible. He was a man on a mission!

According to ICAC, '339 mammals, 32 reptiles, and between 32 and 46 fish specimens' were found missing from the collection after an inventory was conducted in February 2002. The museum referred the matter to ICAC later that year. ICAC investigators found 'strong indicators' that Hank was the culprit. They searched his home and the jig was up.

In September 2003, ICAC released a document titled: 'Report on investigation into the theft of zoological specimens from the Australian Museum between 1997 and 2002 and related matters'. The report included the most amazing excerpts from Hank's interviews with investigators. My personal favourite is this exchange over the theft of the taxidermy lion, which ICAC said was 'illustrative of the audacious nature' of Hank's conduct:

[Counsel Assisting]
Q: The lion?

['Hank']
A: The big stuffed lion. Yes, that came from Marrickville.
Q: From Marrickville?
A: Yes.
Q: And what did you use to get that home?
A: Four wheel drive.
Q: Just put it in the back in this ...?
A: Yes.
Q: ... four wheel drive ...?
A: Yes.
Q: ... and took it home. And what did you do with the lion when you got it home?
A: Cleaned it.
Q: Then what?
A: I had it in my room – in my room.

Q: In your room?

A: Yes.

Q: At home?

A: Yes.

Q: Who for?

A: For me.

Putting a $50,000 stolen lion on display in your bedroom takes 'treating yourself' to a whole new level.

I'm also a massive fan of the following back-and-forth that was included as an example of how Hank stole 'museum property on an opportunistic basis':

[Counsel Assisting]

Q: In 2002 some bats from Western Australia went missing. Do you recall that?

['Hank']

A: I don't know, probably.

Q: You took them, didn't you?

A: What were they?

Q: They were bats.

A: Yeah.

Q: Sent over from a museum in Western Australia. Do you recall last year taking some bats?

A: I recall taking a bag of bats that was laying around, that's all, yeah.

Q: When you say laying around, what do you mean by that?

A: They were just laying around, it's – on a bench or something like that and I just grabbed them.

...

Q: And you saw a bag of bats?

A: Yes.

Q: And helped yourself?

A: And just took them into my office, yeah.

Q: And then took them home?

A: Down the track, yes.

Who can honestly say they wouldn't be tempted by an alluring bag of bats? Then there's this fabulous excerpt from a discussion about packing and transport:

[Counsel Assisting]

Q: ... was it the situation that you would load up a car with a number of items at any one time?

['Hank']

A: I'd take a few, more than one item, yes.

...

Q: Was it a station wagon?

A: No, they were four wheel drives.

Q: Four wheel drives?

A: Yes.

Q: Did you load up the back seat or the rear compartment?

A: Probably the rear compartment, so it depends how many skulls might've fitted in there that I took.

Q: You put in as many skulls as the four wheel drive rear compartment would contain?

A: Yes, most likely I think.

Someone needs to make a YouTube instructional video on how to maximise the skull-to-space ratio when packing zoological specimens into your car (come to think of it, someone probably already has).

The ICAC report unpacked the specifics of Hank's theft campaign. It also made several recommendations for improving the management of the museum's collection. In a way, it was an ideal outcome for Hank, who had so many concerns about the apparent mismanagement of specimens.

A less ideal outcome for Hank was when ICAC sentenced him to seven years in prison, with a non-parole period of five. But Hank wasn't going to let a half-decade jail stint dampen his love of collecting. In an interview with *SBS News* in 2020, he discussed his work in helping to establish a zoological museum in the Central Tablelands of NSW. His personal collection of (legally acquired) specimens would be on display for all Australians to enjoy. As of writing, the museum is still going strong!

When asked about the thefts, Hank confessed to making 'dumb decisions' but insisted his actions were driven by a desire to protect the specimens. Perhaps that's legit. But I'm also inclined to think Robert Mapplethorpe was on the money when he said: 'I don't think any collector knows his true motivation.'

AN ILLICIT SUBSTANCE BY
ANY OTHER NAME

PARENTS OFTEN STRUGGLE TO pick the right name for their child. It's a big responsibility and there are thousands of options to choose from. You don't want to make the wrong decision, like naming your kid 'Dick Stroker' or 'Imma Krapp'. That's what we call 'bad parenting'.

Thankfully, there are laws to prevent Australians from giving their children awful names. The legislation varies from state to state, but the rules are pretty much the same:

1. It can't be more than 50 characters long (e.g. Skylet Antwohnette Lundynn Harmoniegh Knoxlee Princess Tiffany Rampage Jackson).
2. It can't contain phonetic symbols that are 'without significance' or 'unpronounceable' (e.g. J**ckie Kennedy! or Gr@ce Kell%y)
3. It can't include an official title or rank (e.g. His Holiness Sergeant Captain Tom Smith).
4. It can't include a statement (e.g. Kathy is the Queen of the Universe Jones).

5. It must not be in the form of initials or acronyms (e.g. D.J. T.H.O.M.P.S.O.N.).

6. It can't be contrary to the public interest (e.g. Hitler Mussolini Stalin Brown).

7. It must not be obscene or offensive (e.g. Moleface Dickhead Anderson).

In summary, names such as 'Her Majesty M(a)rtha B.R.A.T. diet is good for diarrhoea Butt Features Ku Klux Klan Williams' are off the list. If you apply to register a prohibited name, Birth, Deaths and Marriages will reject your application and ask you to try again.

At least, that's how it's supposed to work. In July 2023, ABC journalist Kirsten Drysdale conducted an experiment for the TV program she was working on to see what would happen if she submitted a completely unacceptable name to New South Wales Births, Deaths and Marriages. She applied to name her newborn son 'Methamphetamine Rules'.

'We thought we would submit the most outrageous name we could think of, assuming it would be rejected,' she told *The Guardian*. (The other name she considered was 'Nangs Rule', with 'nangs' being an Aussie slang term for nitrous oxide canisters. I think she made the right choice.)

So you can imagine Drysdale's surprise when the name was accepted by the state government. 'I was shocked,' she told *SBS News*. 'I thought there must have been a mistake. So I double checked, called them and they said no that's gone through. Then the birth certificate arrived and I knew for sure it had happened.'

NSW Births, Deaths and Marriages admitted the 'unusual name' had been approved in error. The registry took steps to tighten its processes in response to the 'highly unusual event'. They were also working with

Drysdale and her family to correct the mistake. But there was a catch.

'A name registered at birth remains on the NSW Births, Deaths and Marriages Register forever,' a spokesperson for the registry told *The Guardian*. 'Even if the name is formally changed.'

Drysdale hoped her son would share her family's sense of humour about the situation. 'My husband said maybe his nickname should be "Speedy",' she told *The Guardian*.

As for his new name, Drysdale told *SBS News* she was going for something 'very normal' and 'not attached to meth at all'.

BIZARRE LAW #17

Section 8 of the *Summary Offences Act 1966* (Vic) concerns 'offences relating to horse-drawn vehicles, public vehicles, animals etc'. It's a wild piece of legislation that includes a menagerie of unusual offences.

First up, Section 8 prohibits 'driving a cart wagon or dray in or through a public place without the name and residence of the owner thereof being painted in a legible and permanent manner on the right or off side in letters of at least 25 millimetres in length'. I'm assuming this was ye olde version of a number plate? Having your name and address plastered on the side of a wagon sounds like a one-way ticket to identity theft.

It's also an offence to drive 'a dog or goat harnessed or attached to a vehicle in or through a public place'. Does that mean it's okay to have a cat, giraffe or Japanese spider crab harnessed to your vehicle?

Clause (e) penalises anyone who 'sets on, urges or permits a dog or other animal to attack or worry any person, horse or other animal or by ill-usage or negligence in driving cattle causes any mischief to be done by such cattle'. I totally understand the ban on encouraging a dog to attack someone (I've watched *Game of Thrones*), but I'm not so sure about the whole 'worry' thing. A lot of people are 'worried' by rats (including me). Does that mean I can take legal action against anyone who unwittingly shows me their pet rat?

Also, what kind of 'mischief' do cattle get up to? I immediately picture a posse of cows getting wasted on a girl's night out (but maybe that's just me).

Clause (g) bans anyone from slaughtering or skinning 'a beast on a public road or thoroughfare'. Clause (h) bans anyone from leaving 'a dead beast or its skin on a public road or thoroughfare'. Those are two rules I can really get behind.

The final clause prohibits public transport drivers from endangering the lives of passengers 'by reason of intoxication or other misconduct'. (Fair enough.) It also bans them from using 'abusive or insulting language' with passengers, which seems a tad unreasonable. Some passengers deserve a good telling-off. They can be real jackasses.

VENUS VANDALS

A T 11AM ON 3 September 1892, a crowd gathered at the corner of
King William Street and North Terrace in Adelaide to watch the
unveiling of a statue. It was the first public street statue in the history
of the city, so it was a pretty big deal. The marble statue was a copy of
Venere di Canova by the Italian Neoclassical sculptor Antonio Canova,
which depicts Venus, the goddess of love and beauty, emerging from a
bath, partially draped in a sheet (you can totally see her left boob). It
was donated to the City of Adelaide by mining magnate, pastoralist and
politician WA Horn.

The Mayor and Mayoress of Adelaide arrived with an entourage
of dignitaries, including the Premier and the Chief Justice of South
Australia. The Mayor kicked off proceedings by giving a short speech,
before handing over to his wife. According to the *South Australian
Chronicle*: 'The Mayoress then pulled the cord which caused the drapery
to fall away from the Goddess of Beauty, who appeared in all her grace
and loveliness beneath a sky as blue and an atmosphere as clear as were
ever those of Athens or of Paphos.'

Sounds nice!

The Mayor gave a follow-up speech, in which he 'called upon every
citizen to regard himself as a special constable to protect [the] statue

against vandalism'. Sir Edwin Thorn thanked WA Horn for his generosity, saying 'that every citizen, old and young, would join him in
protecting and admiring this beautiful work of art'. The closing remarks
were made by WA Horn himself, who was unfortunately suffering from
a 'severe cold'. He said the statue had been erected in a public park for
the benefit of 'that section of the community which stands most in need
of refining influences'. He invited critics of the statue to 'contemplate
the face of the Venus, and try to realise the aims and the ideals which
animated the sculptor'. The proceedings ended with a toast to the Queen
and the Mayoress. It was all incredibly civilised.

But the statue's 'refining influences' didn't work on everyone. There
was public outcry over the statue's 'indecency', which may explain why
it was temporarily relocated to Adelaide Town Hall two years after the
unveiling. Unfortunately, this wasn't enough to safeguard the statue. On
12 June 1894, *The Express and Telegraph* ran the following story, titled
'THE GODDESS OF BEAUTY. Used as a Hatpeg':

> Apparently all the citizens of Adelaide are not endowed with a rever-
> ence for art. Councillor Packer yesterday complained to the mayor of
> the treatment meted out to Mr. Horn's present to the council ... The
> lady [Venus], it seems, has been temporarily located in the antechamber
> of the Town Hall, and, according to the indignant councillor, people
> attending at the hall 'hang their hats on the statue!' It hardly seems
> in accordance with the eternal fitness of things that Venus should be
> degraded to the level of a common hat stand; so, after passing over
> Alderman Buik's suggestion that the gift should be handed to the
> National Gallery, Mr. Willcox promised to see that the complaint was
> attended to. It may, therefore, be presumed that the Vandals whose
> desecrating hands have been laid upon the statue will discover that its
> object is ornamental and not utilitarian.

The statue was eventually put back on public display, but her troubles were far from over. On 13 July 1925, *The News* reported that the *Venere di Canova* 'apparently offended against the taste of some critics of Adelaide' because someone decided to dress her up in a singlet. (It was the middle of winter – maybe they were just trying to keep her warm.) On 5 June 1928, *The Labor Daily* reported that the statue had been 'decorously draped with a towel'. It's surprising what some people will do to cover up a marble boob.

The next account of Venus vandalism had nothing to do with protecting the statue's modesty. On 26 October 1943, *The Advertiser* reported that the statue had been 'adorned with marigolds and given scarlet toenails'.

But the worst indignity didn't occur until 15 August 1945, when over 1000 people gathered in the city to celebrate the end of the war with Japan. *The Chronicle* ran a story titled 'HOOLIGANISM – Foolish Display in Adelaide', which outlined the various acts of mischief perpetrated by excited 'youths and girls':

> A trail of vandalism was left in the wake of the singing, cheering and whistling crowd each time it made a round of the city streets. Several traffic signs were bent or pushed over, a flagpole snapped in half in front of Parliament House, and milk cans were thrown off trollies at the Railway Station and kicked into King William road.
>
> The Adelaide Arcade, in Rundle street, appeared as if it had been struck by a tornado after the procession had passed through. Stands were tipped over, a fruit counter was opened, and tomatoes, celery and other vegetables were taken from a showcase and pelted at bystanders.

There was also a 'tense scene' outside Elder Park, where a mob of about 300 revellers began throwing 'missiles' at traffic cops. (I'm guessing a few of these 'missiles' were stolen from the Adelaide Arcade's vegetable stands.) Two uniformed police officers stopped the parade at the inter-section of North Terrace and 'told the merrymakers to disperse' (which worked for about ten minutes, until the party reconvened on Rundle Street).

This is where the statue comes in. According to *The Chronicle*, 'a diversion was created by a band of young men who poured kerosene over the statue of Venus ... The kerosene was lit, but the flames petered out in a few seconds'. They turned her into a flambé!

But the goddess of love withstood these slings and arrows with divine grace. Not even arson was enough to knock her off her pedestal. More than a century has passed since the statue was first unveiled, and she's still standing tall. If you're in the vicinity, you can pop down to North Terrace and 'contemplate the face of Venus'. She reminds us not to worry about the haters. You just gotta outlast them.

CLUMSY CAPERS

THE MOVIES OFTEN DEPICT burglars as skilled, stealthy criminals who break into high-security facilities with gymnastic dexterity and technological know-how. Watching Catherine Zeta-Jones weave her way through a web of laser beams in the 1999 blockbuster *Entrapment* makes for great viewing, but it's hardly an accurate portrayal. I'm sorry to say that your average burglar isn't a Welsh goddess with Olympic-level flexibility and a genius IQ. The *Mr Bean* movie is usually closer to reality.

CLUMSY CAPER 1

In December 2006, a 27-year-old thief broke into a pharmacy in Redfern, Sydney with the express purpose of stealing toilet paper. According to *The Daily Telegraph*, 'the man forced his way through the glass doors at the front of the shop ... as he grappled with the iron grill the glass doors shut – and locked – behind him'. He was trapped.

The manager of a nearby pub discovered the accidental prisoner at around 4.30am.

'It was one of the dopiest things I had ever seen,' the publican told *The Daily Telegraph*. 'When I found him he was trying to bash his way out through the bullet proof glass. He asked me to help him get out and I was like "Ah, no".'

The publican notified the cops, who shared the news on the police intercom: 'You might want to come down,' they announced, 'we have the world's dumbest criminal right here.'

The police freed the burglar from his glass enclosure at around 5am. The culprit protested his innocence and begged the officers to stop laughing at him. He said the automatic doors had opened on their own and he'd innocently popped in to have a look. He claimed his alibi was 'watertight'.

Obviously not, because he was arrested and charged with breaking and entering with intent, as well as breaching bail conditions.

CLUMSY CAPER 2

In February 2011, Victoria Police released footage of a bumbling burglar's bizarre bakery break-in. The thief had attempted to rob a bakery in Frankston, Melbourne but accidentally trapped himself in a storeroom. The footage shows the man stacking up bins, boxes, brooms, containers, chairs and shelves in a desperate effort to reach the roof and escape through the storeroom skylight. But indoor climbing wasn't in his skill set, and he ended up crashing to the ground multiple times. The footage also shows him making several phone calls on his mobile, presumably asking for help. He eventually made his way to the skylight, but not without sustaining a nasty gash to his forehead and looking directly into the CCTV camera. The thief knew his bread was baked when the footage was made public, and he surrendered to police.

CLUMSY CAPER 3

In March 2016, Queensland police released CCTV footage of a man breaking into an electronics store in Brisbane. He entered the store via the roof and descended using a rope (*Mission Impossible*–style). I bet he was feeling like a master criminal until he got tangled in the rope, fell off a table and stumbled onto the floor. The unmasked man spent a moment awkwardly putting on his left shoe (which had come unstuck in the process) before he scoped out the shop. The weird thing is that he didn't actually steal anything. (Maybe they didn't have the type of iPad he was after.) There were no stolen items in his loot bag when he began climbing back into the roof. His escape was somewhat hampered when big chunks of the roof started falling around him. Despite these obstacles, and in a true show of resilience, he managed to pull himself up and out of the store (that's some upper-body strength right there).

In summary, the 'thief' broke into a Brisbane electronics store for no apparent reason other than the thrill of haphazardly crawling through a hole in the roof. I guess everyone needs a hobby.

CLUMSY CAPER 4

In June 2017, a 44-year-old man broke into a hotel on Victoria Road in Rozelle, Sydney at around 4.15am. According to *The Daily Mail*, the man made off with cash, documents and a floor safe, which he carried out of the hotel using a shopping trolley. He was discovered by police wheeling the safe along Victoria Road six hours later. Sometimes slow and steady *doesn't* win the race.

CLUMSY CAPER 5

In April 2019, a robbery was committed at a jewellery store in Victoria Park, Perth. Two men wearing motorbike helmets (let's call them 'Laurel' and 'Hardy') broke into the store in the early hours of the morning. CCTV footage showed Laurel entering the store on foot and Hardy following on his motorbike. Laurel appeared moments later carrying a container of jewels. In his haste to escape the crime scene, Laurel tripped on the doorframe and dropped the jewels all over the footpath. He spent a moment picking the scattered booty off the ground and shoving it into his sweatshirt. Half the loot was left lying on the ground when he jumped on the back of the motorbike and drove away with Hardy.

CLUMSY CAPER 6

In May 2021, a man carrying a packet of Maltesers and a bottle of Coke broke into a bar in St Kilda, Melbourne. (It's always a good idea to bring along some snacks when you're committing an indictable offence.) The burglar failed to find any cash in the bar's ATM, so he decided to stock up on alcohol. The general manager of the bar told *9 News* that the thief 'was literally filling up trash bins with booze, looking like he was planning on doing a couple of runs'. But his spirits spree was cut short when the bar boss walked in on him. The thief panicked and leapt from the bar's second-story balcony, landing on his butt.

'He left his Maltesers by the ATM and a bottle of Coke,' said the bar's outgoing general manager. 'Thank you for the Maltesers – I have enjoyed them.'

OUR SERIOUS FROLIC

ACCORDING TO THE AMERICAN poet David Lehman, 'the greatest literary hoax of the twentieth century was concocted by a couple of Australian soldiers at their desks in the offices of the Victoria Barracks in Melbourne ... on a quiet Saturday in October 1943'.

The 'Ern Malley hoax' was the invention of Lieutenant James McAuley and Corporal Harold Stewart. The soldiers were poets who shared a love of classic literature and a hatred of modernist poetry. The pair believed modernist poetry was 'a collection of garish images without coherent meaning and structure'. But the pair wondered if they might be missing something, so they decided to run an experiment.

They decided to manufacture a collection of fake modernist poems by a fake modernist poet and submit them for publication. The question was: would the publishers be able to tell the difference between 'the real product' and 'deliberately concocted nonsense'?

The duo devised a fictional poet named 'Ernest Lalor Malley', who had worked as a garage mechanic and insurance salesperson before tragically passing away at the age of 25 without ever publishing his poems. According to McAuley and Stewart:

We produced the whole of Ern Malley's tragic life-work in one afternoon, with the aid of a chance collection of books which happened to be on our desk: the *Concise Oxford Dictionary*, a *Collected Shakespeare*, *Dictionary of Quotations*, &c.

We opened books at random, choosing a word or phrase haphazardly. We made lists of these and wove them into nonsensical sentences.

We misquoted and made false allusions. We deliberately perpetrated bad verse ...

The first three lines of the poem Culture As Exhibit were lifted, as a quotation, straight from an American report on the drainage of breeding-grounds of mosquitoes.

Once they had completed 17 faux poems (collectively titled *The Darkening Ecliptic*), the duo fabricated 'a very pretentious and meaningless Preface and Statement which purported to explain the aesthetic theory on which they were based'. They wrote up Ern Malley's bio (which took longer than writing the actual poems) and sent two poems to Max Harris, an arts student at the University of Adelaide who co-founded the Australian literary journal *Angry Penguins*. They sent the poems from 'Ethel Malley' – Ern's equally fake sister. A letter was enclosed from 'Ethel' asking Harris if he could see any value in her late brother's poetry. Here's a sample from Malley's poem 'Sonnets for the Novachord':

Though stilled to alabaster
This Ichthys shall swim
From the mind's disaster
On the volatile hymn.
If this be the norm
Of our serious frolic
There's no remorse:
Our magical force

Cleaves the ignorant storm
On the hyperbolic.

Harris was enraptured by Malley's verse. He was convinced he had discovered one of the 'two giants of contemporary Australian poetry'. Harris published all 17 of Malley's poems in the June 1944 edition of *Angry Penguins*, along with a glowing introduction. Other fans of modernist poetry got on the bandwagon, including Brian Elliott, a lecturer in Australian Literature from the University of Adelaide. A selection of Malley's poems was also included in an anthology of Australian verse published in New York. The experiment had worked.

The hoax was revealed three weeks later when a statement from McAuley and Stewart was published in *FACT* magazine. In the statement, they explained why and how they had invented Ern Malley. They also discussed why intelligent people were convinced by the sham. They argued that Harris and the like were so 'hypnotised' by the 'cultism' of the modernist movement that it suspended 'the operation of [their] critical intelligence'. They concluded by saying (just in case there was any doubt) that 'the Writings of Ern Malley [were] utterly devoid of literary merit'.

When *FACT* magazine called Harris for comment, he insisted that 'whoever wrote the Ern Malley poems was a fine poet'. He said the editors of *Angry Penguins* 'were satisfied with the intrinsic merits of the verse'.

News of the 'Ern Malley hoax' spread throughout Australia and abroad. The story was featured in *The Times* (London) and *Time* magazine. Despite his ongoing faith in the merits of Malley's poetry, Harris became an international laughing-stock.

To make matters worse, he was also hit with a court case. South Australian police were scandalised by the sexual references in Ern Malley's poems and charged Harris with publishing 'indecent' material. The cops didn't appreciate the use of words such as 'bugger', 'pubic', 'concupiscence', 'genitals' and 'incestuous'. They also didn't appreciate phrases such as 'you can stick it' and 'part of me remains wench, Boult-upright, the rest of me drops off into the night'.

Harris pleaded not guilty at his hearing at the Adelaide Police Court on 5 September 1944. Several literary expert witnesses gave testimony in support of *Angry Penguins*. The only witness for the prosecution was Detective Jacobus Vogelesang. According to the *Northern Star* news-paper, the detective 'thought the word incestuous was indecent, but he did not know what it meant'. Vogelesang believed it was 'immoral' to discuss sex with his friends, so I'm guessing he was a real laugh-a-minute down at the pub. He reportedly asked Harris about the negative effects of Ern Malley's poetry on high school children. Harris clapped back by saying 'the Bible could have a worse effect'. (Probably not the best thing to say to a police officer in the City of Churches.)

Harris was found guilty. He was given a suspended sentence and charged £5 (equivalent to A$440). *Angry Penguins* never recovered from the scandal and ceased publication in 1946.

But the story of Ern Malley didn't end there.

Over the years, Australia's greatest non-existent poet has inspired more creative output than any other non-existent poet in recorded history. The internationally acclaimed painter Sir Sidney Nolan was a prominent enthusiast. He held an exhibition called 'Ern Malley and Paradise Garden' in 1974, painted a 'self-portrait' of Ern Malley and credited the fictional poet with inspiring his renowned Ned Kelly series. Various authors, poets and playwrights have referenced Malley in their work, including Peter Carey, who based his award-winning novel *My Life as a Fake* on the Ern Malley hoax.

Several academics and critics have also argued that the poems are much better than the authors ever intended. In 2011, Associate Professor of English at the University of Sydney, David Brooks, spoke to *The Sydney Morning Herald* about the merits of Malley's verse. 'The poems possess depths revealing deeper forces at work rather than just being something casually tossed off by a couple of schoolyard bullies one afternoon,' said Brooks. 'They are far from the gibberish or nonsense poems of popular belief. There are references to Shakespeare, Keats ... it's all so carefully constructed.' It's a shame Associate Professor Brooks wasn't around to give Detective Vogelesang a short course on English literature (or at least explain to him what the word 'incestuous' means).

As for the maligned Max Harris, he didn't stay maligned for long. He launched a literary magazine called *Ern Malley's Journal* in 1951 (which is a totally kickass thing to do). He forged a successful career as a bookseller, critic, editor, poet and newspaper columnist. He received the Order of Australia and was awarded the title of 'Father of Modernism in the Australian Arts' by the University of Adelaide. He remained a devoted fan of the invented poet until his death in 1995.

In the words of Ern Malley, 'there's no remorse'.

ARIARIA DRAMARAMIAS

THE AUSTRALIAN RECORDING INDUSTRY Association Music Awards (better known as 'the ARIAs') is our nation's answer to the Grammy Awards. It's the night when Australia's music industry comes together to celebrate its best and brightest. Since they commenced in 1987, the ARIAs have been graced by the likes of Elton John, Dolly Parton, Harry Styles, Olivia Newton-John, Robbie Williams, Taylor Swift and Sporty Spice. It's a night to remember, but not always for the right reasons.

It's fair to say that the 2010 ARIAs were a total dumpster fire. I don't know what went wrong in the production process, but the choice to host the event on the steps of the Sydney Opera House (rather than *inside* the Sydney Opera House) did not pan out well. The crowds of celebrities standing and sipping booze made it difficult for anyone to make themselves heard. Co-host Natalie Bassingthwaighte spent most of the evening screaming into the camera. As journalist David Knox remarked, the presenters were 'awkwardly staged like gate crashers, [and] frequently shot from low angles with shadows cast every time somebody moved'. The 'shambolic' atmosphere seemed to increase the incidence of presenter screw-ups. Right-wing Queensland politician Bob Katter (I don't understand why he was even there) referred to the event as the 'ARIARIAs'.

Meanwhile, singer Jessica Mauboy repeatedly mispronounced 'debut' as 'de-butt' (which I'm sure still haunts her to this day).

Reflecting on the shitshow a year later, music blogger David Larkin summed up the audience reaction perfectly: 'So gross was last year's "stubby-on-the-opera-house-steps" screaming match, that it still burns a brutal reflux just thinking what horrible depths our embattled industry and its unfortunate viewership plummeted to on that grievous evening of small screen hell.'

As dreadful as it was, the 2010 ARIAs didn't break any actual laws (unfortunately, poor event planning isn't illegal). The same can't be said of the 2007 ARIAs, which became the centre of a scandal after *Media Watch* ran a segment accusing the producers of 'subliminal advertising'.

Subliminal advertising was invented in 1957 by American marketing researcher James Vicary. He claimed to have significantly increased cinema sales of Coca-Cola and popcorn by inserting single-frame advertisements into movies, saying 'Drink Coca-Cola' and 'Eat Popcorn'. The ads only appeared for one three-thousandth of a second, which is too fast for most people to consciously perceive. Vicary alleged that the advertisements worked on a 'subliminal' level, influencing the consumer's subconscious mind.

News of Vicary's invention caused widespread panic and outrage. The idea of being influenced by unconscious messages didn't sit well with people. One American magazine even compared subliminal advertising to the dystopian tyranny of George Orwell's *1984*. Governments and regulatory bodies around the world quickly made moves to outlaw this form of marketing mind control. In 1958, the American National Association of Broadcasters banned subliminal advertising. Britain and Australia followed suit. Subliminal advertising is now prohibited in Australia under Schedule 2 of the *Competition and Consumer Act 2011* (Cth) and the Commercial Television Industry Code of Practice (just in case you were wondering).

In 1962, Vicary confessed that the subliminal advertising palaver had been a publicity stunt to promote his marketing company. He never had any meaningful evidence supporting his claims, and there are questions over whether he ever conducted experiments at all. Since then, there have been several scientific studies looking at the impact of subliminal messages. *Scientific American* published a piece summarising these findings in 2012. It found that 'subliminal messaging is far less potent or terrifying than it was first believed to be'. While it can have some degree of influence, several mitigating factors stop subliminal advertising from turning us into consumer zombies. The article concludes that 'our subconscious registers many different kinds of suggestions, not just the ones advertisers may be aiming for'.

It's hard to say what the producers of the 2007 ARIAs were aiming for with their advertising strategy, but it wasn't good. They decided to intersperse the nominee announcements with company logos that flashed up for one twenty-fifth of a second. For example, the nominations for best female artist went like this:

Announcer: Kate Miller-Heidke, 'Little Eve'.
OLAY logo flashes up for 0.04 seconds
Announcer: Missy Higgins, 'On a Clear Night'.
OLAY logo flashes up for 0.04 seconds

Other briefly featured logos included BigPond, Chupa Chups, KFC and Toyota.

In response to *Media Watch's* criticism, as well as complaints from viewers, the Australian Communications and Media Authority (ACMA) launched an investigation. Network Ten denied the allegations, saying that the quick cuts were designed to imitate the feel of a music video clip and were never intended as 'subliminal or near subliminal advertising'. ACMA didn't buy this excuse, stating that the ads were 'below normal awareness' and had been inserted with 'considerable precision'. Network Ten was found in breach of the code of practice and had to jump through several hoops to appease ACMA. This included distributing the investigation report to relevant production staff, conducting regular code of practice training sessions and highlighting the code clause in its external production agreements. Network Ten also promised to avoid the use of rapid cuts in the 2008 ARIAs.

I just feel sorry for the poor souls at the network who were tasked with all the extra admin. It sounds like a real pain in de-butt.

THE BONK BAN

WHILE THERE ARE NO actual crimes described in this chapter (unless you consider adultery, hypocrisy and stupidity crimes), this is the story of a 'law' created in unusual, entertaining and illuminating circumstances. So much 'bizarreness' surrounds this case that it had to make the cut. Also, the opportunity to make fun of the politicians concerned was too tempting to pass up.

National Party stalwart and career politician Barnaby Joyce was always a vocal opponent of marriage equality. As a married Roman Catholic with four daughters, Barnaby was committed to a 'traditional' view of marriage. In an interview in 2015, he told *ABC Insiders* that recognising same-sex marriage would be equivalent to saying 'a diamond is a square'. He also worried that Asian countries would see Australia as 'decadent' if the nation redefined marriage. 'I see marriage as a reflection of what I have, what my parents had, what my grandparents had,' he told the *ABC*. 'It's not about equality.'

Fast forward to 7 February 2018. *The Daily Telegraph* published an exposé claiming that Barnaby was having a baby with his former deputy chief of staff Vikki Campion. The article was titled 'BUNDLE OF JOYCE' (which is pure genius) and showcased a photo of a heavily pregnant Campion walking near her home in Canberra. It reported that

50-year-old Barnaby was 'madly in love' with 33-year-old Campion and the couple were expecting their newborn in April.

Barnaby's wife Natalie Joyce released a statement saying she was 'deeply saddened' by the news. 'This affair has been going on for many months and started when she was a paid employee,' she said. 'Naturally we feel deceived and hurt by the actions of Barnaby and the staff member involved.' (It's a shame she didn't call her husband's behaviour 'decadent' – that would have been a full-circle moment.)

Soon after, Barnaby announced he was stepping down as deputy prime minister and leader of the National Party. He would remain in parliament, but only as a backbencher. He said his removal from the political spotlight would give 'clear air' to his party.

In an interview with *The Sydney Morning Herald*, the embattled MP called into question the paternity of Campion's child (plot twist!). The baby was conceived between June and July 2017, when Barnaby was either travelling overseas with his wife or 'accompanied by close personal protection bodyguards'. This made it difficult to figure out when the 'baby making' might have occurred. (You try juggling an illicit affair with a staff member while travelling with your wife and platforming a 'family values' political agenda – it's logistically very challenging.)

Barnaby said the child's paternity was 'a bit of a grey area' and criticised *The Daily Telegraph* for jumping to conclusions. 'How could they know' he said. 'They never even asked if it was Joyce's bundle.' (The journalist must have assumed Barnaby and Campion were in a monogamous relationship, which I must admit is quite presumptuous. If National Party members are known for anything, it's their libertine attitudes to sexual experimentation and polyamory.)

Nevertheless, he was committed to raising Campion's child, regardless of biology. 'It's mine, on the record, there it is,' he said. 'And can I say, even if it wasn't, I wouldn't care, I'd still go through this, I'd still love him.' So why did he bring up the paternity question if he was planning on claiming the baby as his own? I have no idea.

Amid this soap opera insanity, Prime Minister Malcolm Turnbull gave a speech condemning Barnaby's actions. 'I think we know that the real issue is the terrible hurt and humiliation that Barnaby by his conduct has visited on his wife, Natalie, and their daughters, and indeed, his new partner,' said Turnbull. 'Barnaby made a shocking error of judgment in having an affair with a young woman working in his office. In doing so he has set off a world of woe for those women and appalled all of us.'

In the 2023 *Sky News* documentary 'Liberals in Power: Part One', Barnaby recalls watching Turnbull's speech on television and saying, 'What's this dipstick up to?'

'This dipstick' was announcing a formal ban on any ministers engaging in sexual relations with their staff 'regardless of whether they are married or single'. This update to the ministerial standards was immediately labelled the 'bonk ban'.

You might think conservative politicians would welcome a prohibition on sexually inappropriate workplace relations, but apparently not.

One vocal opponent of the ban was Victorian National MP Andrew Broad. 'It sends a message to the Australian people that the Parliament is somehow an incestuous orgy, and it just isn't,' he said in an interview on Melbourne radio. Broad resigned later that year after *New Idea* published a story revealing the married politician had 'been caught out with a sugar baby from a "seeking arrangements" website he used to meet younger girls while he was away on work trips'. The 'sugar baby' in question used the online name 'Sweet Sophia Rose' and said the MP had 'bragged about his "important" position in parliament, practised his official speeches and even referred to himself as "James Bond" in an attempt to seduce her'. (I struggle to imagine James Bond serving as the representative for Mallee.) Broad reportedly sent 'Sweet Sophia Rose' a flurry of texts, including one that read: 'I'm an Aussie lad, I know how to ride a horse, fly a plane and f—k my woman. My intentions are completely dishonourable.'

Did someone say something about an orgy?

Six months after the bonk ban was announced, Turnbull was ousted in a leadership spill. Barnaby believed Turnbull's response to the sex scandal was instrumental in his downfall. 'This is an incredibly bombastic egotistical statement,' Barnaby said in an interview with Chris Kenny, 'but it's the truth [that] when he lost me, he lost.' (I'm inclined to agree with the first part of that statement.)

Coalition MPs with a taste for workplace liaisons must have been disappointed when newly installed Prime Minister Scott Morrison continued to back the ban, saying it was 'the right thing to do'.

Barnaby and Campion were married in November 2023 at a 'bush bash' wedding in the NSW Northern Tablelands, which one guest compared to 'a bachelor and spinster ball'. *The Daily Telegraph* reported that the bride and groom wore Barnaby's 'trademark Akubra country hats' and Campion praised Barnaby as a 'family man' in her vows. The couple's two young sons – aged four and five – served as pageboys. Barnaby's four daughters from his first marriage were notably absent.

Before the big day, Barnaby's 24-year-old daughter Julia posted an Instagram video of her wearing her mother's wedding dress. The caption said: 'Getting ready to crash my dad's wedding I didn't get invited to, in my mum's wedding dress.' (I'm sad to report that she didn't follow through on this threat. I wish she had. My life would have been complete.) Meanwhile, her 20-year-old sister Odette told *The Daily Mail* that her father hadn't even told her about the upcoming nuptials. 'I found out through other sources,' she said. 'If my father doesn't want to think about me or even consider me in the decisions he makes that ultimately affect me then frankly I don't have the time to think about him.'

It's interesting to reflect that divorce was rarely recognised under English or Australian law until the mid-19th century. Before then, it was extremely difficult to get divorced, let alone legally remarry. Barnaby can thank his lucky stars that laws and attitudes have changed with time. In truth, we should all be thankful. It's a beautiful thing to marry the person you love, regardless of whether you're a diamond or a square.

A FORK IN THE ROAD

SHOUTING 'STOP! THIEF!' ISN'T always the most effective strategy when it comes to stopping thieves. Indeed, thieves sometimes go to great lengths to avoid capture and equally great lengths are required to stop them in their tracks.

Brisbane man Brendan Mills took thief-catching to a whole new level in June 2022 when he arrived home with his family to discover a woman attempting to steal his Volkswagen Polo. The 24-year-old thief had already broken into the Mills's home, where she took a shower and changed her clothes. (It's nice to freshen up before committing grand theft auto.)

'I asked them many times to get out of the car: "We're home, you're busted. Get out the car, you know it's over",' he told *BBC Australia*. 'They didn't want to get out.'

But the thief hadn't reckoned with Brendan's ingenuity – or the industrial vehicle parked in his driveway.

'You had this immense amount of adrenaline running through the system, lots of thoughts cross your mind,' he said. 'I just went, "Well, there's a forklift sitting there – why not?"' (I'm not entirely sure why Brendan had a forklift in the driveway, but just roll with me on this one.)

Brendan jumped into his forklift and swiftly lifted the Volkswagen.

The position of the forks meant the thief couldn't use the car doors to escape. She was trapped in a bright red, German-engineered prison hanging in the air.

The car was finally lowered when the cops arrived. An officer opened the front passenger door and said 'out you get' to the defeated fugitive. Police video shows her sitting on the ground, handcuffed and cross-legged, looking forlorn.

A Queensland police statement revealed that the thief was charged with burglary and unlawful use of an automobile. The statement also issued a gentle warning: 'To ensure community safety, police recommend members of the public not engage in methods of disrupting criminal activity which may involve risk of personal harm or further legal recourse.' Fair enough. Using a forklift isn't the most 'sensible' approach. But it's hard to criticise Brendan when he has such an uplifting story.

HUMOUR AND CONTEMPT

T HE IDEA FOR A bridge over Sydney Harbour was first suggested by the convict architect Francis Greenway in 1815. Several proposals were made throughout the 19th century, but things didn't get serious until 1900, when a design competition was called by the NSW Government and civil engineer Dr JJC Bradfield became involved. Bradfield was appointed chief engineer of the project in 1912, and construction of the 52,800-tonne steel arch bridge got underway in 1923. Over 1600 people were involved in the nine-year build, which was completed in early 1932, 117 years after the idea was first floated.

Anticipation was at an all-time high as over a quarter of a million people gathered for the opening ceremony at 10am on Saturday 19 March 1932. According to *The Beaudesert Times*, 'an atmosphere of gaiety and splendid pageantry' surrounded the long-awaited occasion. 'Glorious sunshine flooded the harbour' and ships on the water were 'gay with bunting'. Crowds of onlookers had arrived 'after midnight, and spent the night in the open to make sure of front places at the points of vantage'. (It was the 1930s maritime equivalent of a Taylor Swift concert.)

The NSW Labor Premier John 'Jack' Lang received a thunderous ovation when he arrived to perform the ceremony. The Governor-General, the State Governor and other dignitaries were in attendance.

Everything was set for an ideal opening. But just as Lang was about to cut the ceremonial ribbon with 'an historic pair of scissors', a man dressed in military uniform charged out of the crowd on horseback and cut the ribbon with a sword. He declared the bridge open in the name of 'the decent and respectable people of New South Wales'. The Premier's thunder was stolen, and the premature ribbon-cutter was dragged away by police.

The renegade bridge opener was a 43-year-old Irishman named Francis Edward de Groot. De Groot had served with the 15th Hussars in World War I before moving to Sydney in 1920 and setting up a high-end furniture business. In 1931, he became a member of the 'New Guard' – a proto-fascist paramilitary organisation established by the far-right extremist and lawyer Eric Campbell. The New Guard was dedicated to disrupting leftist meetings and had an axe to grind with the proudly socialist Premier Lang. They were outraged by Lang's decision to open the Sydney Harbour Bridge himself, rather than inviting a member of the Royal Family to perform the ceremony. (There was also drama about unpaid interest payments to overseas investors, but my interest dropped off a cliff when I started to look into it.) The New Guard swore to stop Lang from opening the bridge and there were legitimate concerns they would kidnap the Premier before the big day.

Despite de Groot's best efforts, Lang was still the official 'opener' of the Sydney Harbour Bridge. Officials repaired the ribbon and the Premier cut it with his 'historic pair of scissors'. There was an aerial salute executed by 12 Air Force planes 'which dived close on to the bridge with a tremendous roar from a great height'. Speeches were made and the crowds were witness to 'an amazing procession on a stupendous scale'. The proto-fascists had failed to derail the 'gaiety' of the day.

Meanwhile, de Groot was taken to the Darlinghurst reception centre under suspicion of being 'insane'. One of the arresting officers was quoted saying: 'I never had any experience of arresting an insane man on horseback.' There was speculation that the 'insanity' accusation was just a pointed effort by the police to undermine the New Guard, but nobody knows for sure. After psychiatrists determined that de Groot was not 'insane', he was arrested. According to *The Brisbane Courier*, he was charged on three counts:

1. having maliciously damaged a ribbon, the property of the New South Wales Government, to the extent of £2
2. having behaved in an offensive manner at the junction of Bradfield Highway and the Sydney Harbour Bridge, a public place
3. having used the threatening words – 'I am a King's officer; stand back; don't you interfere with me' – to Inspector Stuart Robson, in a public place.

De Groot appeared before Sydney's Central Police Court on 22 March 1932 and pled not guilty to all charges. According to *The Brisbane Courier,* there was 'great public interest' in the case and the 'court corridors were densely crowded'. *The Telegraph* reported that New Guard founder Eric Campbell was serving as the defendant's solicitor. (As a rule, it's ill-advised to have the leader of a fascist organisation as your legal counsel.) The court was told that the unauthorised ribbon cutting 'was designed to combine humour with contempt'. The defendant justified his actions by attacking Premier Lang's politics:

Captain de Groot said he had a strong motive for his act in the policy of Mr. Lang, which had, he believed, the object of 'Sovietising' New South Wales in a constitutional manner as a prelude to the 'Sovietisation' of the Commonwealth. Upon such political motives, said de Groot, contempt should be poured.

The Telegraph mentioned that de Groot had 'received thousands of telegrams of congratulations from all parts of Australia'. There was also a 'de Groot fund' set up to 'commemorate his action'. To top it off, members of the New Guard presented de Groot with a hand-painted flag in celebration of his not-so-grand opening. (I wonder if the proto-fascist militia painted the flag at their weekly craft meet-up group?)

He was granted bail and returned to court on 6 April for sentencing. Magistrate Laidlaw was unconvinced by the 'reds under the bed' argument and found the defendant guilty of offensive behaviour in a public place (but dismissed the 'ribbon cutting' and 'threatening words' charges). The magistrate described de Groot's actions as 'grossly offensive, provocative and clearly unlawful'. He also accused de Groot of 'showing disrespect to the King's representatives', which must have felt like a kick in the balls to the staunch monarchist. Laidlaw issued the maximum fine of £5 with £4 costs (equivalent to A$1070) in default of 18 days of prison with hard labour.

The 'de Groot incident' quickly turned into a running joke (or, in this case, a 'galloping joke'), with de Groot impersonators appearing at ribbon-cutting ceremonies across the country. *The Grenfell Record and Lachlan District Adviser* reported one such incident at a road opening in May 1933:

> The official opening of the recently gazetted Hervely's Range (Q.) road was performed on Sunday week last, when, in the presence of a large gathering ... A touch of comedy was added to the proceedings when a district tobacco grower re-acted the De Groot incident at the opening of the Sydney Harbor Bridge. Dashing on horseback, the De Groot impersonator, with cowboy yells, scattered the crowd gathered around the stretched ribbon, which he severed, at full gallop, with a large knife. Digging spurs into his mount 'De Groot the Second' then galloped off

into the bush. The ribbon was replaced, and later was severed officially by Mrs. Wordworth, wife of the Shire Chairman.

The original de Groot was back in the news in July 1932 after he was caught driving across the Sydney Harbour Bridge with an 'insufficient tail light' and fined five shillings. He was back in the news again in November 1932 when he sued the NSW Police for 'wrongful arrest'. He claimed £5000 in damages but settled out of court for £68. Once we factor in the fines for offensive behaviour and a dodgy tail light, he turned a profit of over £58 (equivalent to A$6900). He also scored a hand-crafted flag. Talk about making out like a bandit!

De Groot soon broke his association with Eric Campbell (smart move) and returned to the high-end furniture business. He served in World War II (fighting *against* the Nazis this time) and passed away in a Dublin nursing home in 1969. *The Canberra Times* reported his passing with the headline: 'NEW GUARD' – 'HUSSAR' DIES IN DUBLIN. According to the report, de Groot's death went unnoticed in his homeland of Ireland 'where he was little known'. But his memory lived on Down Under, where he was still 'famed in Australian history for unofficially opening the Sydney Harbour Bridge'. It proved to be the defining moment of his chequered life.

In 2004, de Groot was back in the news *again* when Associate Professor Andrew Moore of the University of Western Australia revealed that he knew the whereabouts of de Groot's infamous sword. After mentioning the sword in a talk at University College, Dublin, Professor Moore was approached by a man who turned out to be de Groot's nephew Frank. Frank took the professor to his farm in County Wicklow where the sword was located. *The Age* reported that the National Museum of Australia was 'confident' they would win the bid for this sharp slice of Aussie history.

But in 2007 it was revealed that the museum had been outbid by Paul

Cave, the owner of BridgeClimb – a company that helps people climb to the top of the Sydney Harbour Bridge. Cave told *The Daily Telegraph* he had paid a 'significant' amount for the ribbon-slashing relic, which he described as 'very, very special'. He claimed to have looked for the elusive object for 18 years, including placing ads that read: 'Wanted: the sabre that rattled a premier and astonished a city.'

The sword was kept in a wooden box inscribed with the motto 'swords are stronger than scissors'. They're also more memorable.

I'M WITH STUPID

I N 2015, THE STATE Library of Queensland acquired an 'I'm With Stupid' T-shirt for the John Oxley research collection of 'electoral ephemera'. Given the colourful and eccentric history of Queensland politics, nobody should be surprised that an 'I'm With Stupid' T-shirt found its way into the election spin cycle. In a way, it was inevitable.

On the morning of 8 January 2015, 44-year-old Iain Fogerty arrived at Brunswick Street in Fortitude Valley, Brisbane wearing an 'I'm With Stupid' T-shirt he purchased online for US$7.99. Brunswick Street was a political battleground between the rival Liberal National Party of Queensland (LNP) and Labor Party candidates campaigning in the lead-up to the Queensland state election on 31 January 2015. Fogerty – who was a staunch opponent of sitting Liberal Party Premier Campbell Newman and the creator of the popular parody Twitter account @Can_Do_Campbell – came to support Labor candidate Grace Grace and undermine LNP Member for Brisbane Central Robert Cavallucci.

At around 8.30am, police began to receive complaints of someone creating a disturbance on Brunswick Street. Young LNP members had accused Fogerty of acting 'aggressively' and 'pushing people around'. In what has since been described as an 'over-reaction', no less than ten officers arrived on the scene and arrested Fogerty.

Grace Grace's campaign manager Judi Jabour was outraged by the arrest. She claimed Fogerty had done nothing wrong. He was simply standing next to LNP volunteers and posing for photos. 'All he was doing was standing there waving with an "I'm with Stupid" T-shirt on,' Jabour told *Brisbane Times*.

Fogerty was charged with creating a 'public nuisance' and put on 'watchhouse bail'. A Queensland police spokesperson maintained that the arrest 'didn't have anything to do with the shirt'.

Of course, social media users delighted in making fun of the incident. @ABCnewsintern tweeted: '"I'm with stupid" is clear provocation of Queensland police who must enforce strict association laws.' @MrTimCallanan tweeted: 'Man arrested at a campaign event in Qld, wearing "I'm With Stupid" T-shirt ... thus getting the campaign officially underway #qldvotes.' The hashtag #ImWithStupid was trending, and the story gained international attention.

It's hard to say if the 'I'm With Stupid' T-shirt incident had any impact on the state election results, but Fogerty must have been chuffed with the outcome. Robert Cavallucci lost his seat to Grace Grace and Campbell Newman lost his top job to Annastacia Palaszczuk. Labor scraped through with a minority government, but it was still a win.

Fogerty scored another win when the case against him was dropped after police failed to produce any evidence and Magistrate Christopher Callaghan dismissed the charges on 4 March 2015. He told *Brisbane Times* that he was 'never afraid or worried' about the arrest or court case. 'I was more amused by the whole event,' he said, adding that he 'lay no blame at the feet of police'.

The avid Labor supporter was less charitable when it came to the Young LNP members who dobbed him into the cops. Fogerty called them 'politically naïve' and questioned their ability to withstand the harsh realities of political life: 'If they are unable to cope with someone wearing a shirt with a dumb slogan, then they are clearly not suitable to cope with the far greater pressure that politics will bring,' he said. 'I suggest they find a hobby more suitable to their delicate nature and leave elections to those with a more robust spine.'

Fogerty said he was glad to hand over his T-shirt to the State Library, although he did find the whole situation 'quite bizarre'. Meanwhile, State Library of Queensland coordinator Brian Randall saw genuine value in the acquisition. Randall said 'the "I'm With Stupid" t-shirt would join other famous political T-shirts like "Kevin 07" and "Joh for PM".'

'In itself it's an example of how people were sending a message, and maybe a protest,' he told *Brisbane Times*. 'In the future historians will look at it and think OK, why was this used, how was it used – it's part of the colour of the election.'

When historians look back at the history of Queensland politics, there will be no shortage of colour.

THE TACO VAN FOR JACKIE CHAN
THE RAM

O N Boxing Day 2016, a 51-year-old man (let's call him 'Isaac') stole a pop-up mobile taco van from Torquay, Victoria. Isaac hooked the $65,000 van to his car and drove it back to a property in Melton. He didn't steal the van in hopes of setting up his own black-market taco truck business. Rather, he wanted to turn the van into a residence for his nine-year-old pet ram, Jackie Chan. He gutted the van and removed all taco-related 'stickers and insignia' to prepare it as sleeping quarters for himself and his large horned male sheep.

Isaac and Jackie Chan the ram had been doing 'protest rounds' in Canberra just before the taco van heist. Isaac was protesting an order from Moorabool Shire Council to remove Jackie Chan from his Bacchus Marsh property after the animal was accused of attacking people. Moorabool Mayor Allan Comrie told *The Age* that the issue of Isaac's ram had been a 'saga'. 'It's been going on for years,' he said. 'The residents, his neighbours, are really suffering. Rams are dangerous animals – they're like bulls, they'll butt anyone if they can.' The council gave Isaac a deadline to find the ram a new home or they would take possession. The council assured Isaac that the creature would be kept somewhere safe where he could visit him, but Isaac was worried it would be 'lights out' for Jackie Chan.

Isaac chose to leave his property rather than surrender his beloved companion, and the duo spent part of 2016 sleeping rough on a grassed traffic island in Melbourne's CBD. *The Age* reported that Jackie Chan received a much-needed haircut in a park opposite the Immigration Museum in May 2016. When they interviewed Isaac, he discussed his ongoing campaign against the council. 'Moorabool wiped their hands of me so I'm now the Melbourne Mayor's problem,' he said.

According to the *Geelong Advertiser*, Isaac took Jackie Chan 'on a trip to Canberra and Parliament House hoping to take his woolly issue to a federal level'. He wanted Prime Minister Malcolm Turnbull to over-turn the council's decision and the ram to be registered as a 'companion animal'. Isaac's lobbying proved fruitless, and he was worse for wear by the time he got back to Victoria. At his hearing at Geelong Magistrate's Court in March 2007, he admitted to being less than lucid when he stole the van.

'By the time I came to my senses and realised what had happened I was in panic stations,' he told Magistrate Frank Jones. 'I didn't quite know what to do, to be honest, your honour.'

Magistrate Jones showed a keen interest in Jackie Chan's wellbeing and made some interesting sheep-related remarks. 'I thought the wool prices were pretty good at the moment,' said the magistrate. 'You could have done some of the spinning yourself ... You don't hire him out at all do you?'

Isaac answered that he had hired Jackie Chan out in the past but 'it is mating season and I'm having a bit of trouble with him'. (I shudder to think what 'trouble' with a pet ram looks like during mating season.)

The defendant expressed remorse over the theft. 'I'm disgusted in myself that I've done it,' said Isaac. 'I'm outraged, I can't believe I did something like that.' (The ram's thoughts on the matter were not reported.)

Magistrate Jones conceded that Isaac was suffering from health problems that impacted his decision-making. He decided against incarceration and sentenced Isaac to a 12-month community corrections order, as well as 150 hours of unpaid community service (which was reduced to a $900 fine a month later).

Despite his leniency, the magistrate also stressed the negative consequences of Isaac's actions. 'You actually ruined [the taco truck owners'] life ... you put him out of business forever,' he said. 'You've got a lot of publicity about you and your ram but people ... will not like this.'

It was a sorry end to the tale of the taco van for Jackie Chan the ram.

THE WITCH OF KINGS CROSS

Rosaleen Norton was born at night – in a raging thunderstorm – in Dunedin, New Zealand, on 2 October 1917. The newborn had naturally pointed ears and dark spots on her knees, physical characteristics that would have been 'marks of the devil' in centuries past. It was a fitting start for the woman who would later be known as 'the witch of Kings Cross'.

After throwing off the shackles of her conservative Church of England childhood (she was expelled from Chatswood Girls Grammar at the age of 14 for being a 'corrupting influence' when she shared 'depraved' drawings of vampires and werewolves with her classmates), Norton moved to Sydney where she studied art and joined the bohemian scene. She worked as a journalist, kitchen hand, nightclub wait staffer and postie, and modelled for the famed Australian artist Norman Lindsay. She explored self-hypnosis, psychedelics, pagan ritual, Jewish mysticism, western occultism, eastern esotericism and 'sex magic'. By the later 1940s, her life as a witch was fully underway.

Norton had her first art exhibition at the Rowden White Library, University of Melbourne, in August 1949. The exhibition showcased paintings and drawings of pagan deities, demons and supernatural entities, often depicted in sexually suggestive poses. The works included such titles as 'Lucifer' and 'Witches' Sabbath'. This was all *extremely* controversial for Menzies-era Australia, so it wasn't a huge surprise when the cops showed up, seized four of the paintings and charged Norton with 'obscenity'. Surprisingly, the case was dismissed after Norton had a chance to explain her artwork in court. But the controversy caught the public's eye, and they weren't about the forget the artistic witch from Kings Cross.

Things really blew up in 1952 with the release of the book *The Art of Rosaleen Norton*, which featured Norton's artwork alongside poems written by Sydney bohemian Gavin Greenlees (who was Norton's constant companion until he was institutionalised with schizophrenia in 1955). The book inspired instant outrage and drew the ire of tabloid media.

On 7 September 1952, *The Sunday Sun* ran a hatchet piece titled: 'They wanted to bind it in batskin. Witches, demons on rampage in weird Sydney sex book.' The article began: 'Sex symbolism is portrayed with such stark abandon in a strictly-limited edition of an art work just published in Sydney that an all-male staff of book-binders was engaged to bind the work.' The article alleges that the book was originally going to be bound in bat skin until Norton nixed that idea because she 'objected to the killing of bats'. The report describes the scandalous nature of the artwork, which featured 'grotesque human figures with upper halves of women and lower halves of men'. The images included 'demons, skulls, serpents, erotic emblems and religious symbols', as well as 'pictorial lampoons of bishops and other churchmen, including a naked priest'. The imagery used 'was that associated with medieval cult of the Witches' Sabat'.

The Sunday Sun homed in on an image titled 'Black Magic', which showed a naked woman embracing a panther. The image scandalised Mrs D Woodward, vice-president of the Progressive Housewives' Association. Mrs Woodward apparently took one look at 'Black Magic' and asked the reporter of *The Sunday Sun* how much the book cost. She was relieved when she learned that the book cost eight guineas (equivalent to A$375). 'Thank heavens,' she exclaimed. 'Price will keep it out of harm's way.'

Never one to back down from controversy, Norton agreed to be interviewed by *The Sunday Sun*:

> Rosaleen Norton herself, sitting cross-legged on a couch in a Kings Cross room, sipping sherry and smoking cigarettes, disagreed with her critics.
>
> She denied her drawings contained any sexuality, and rifled through the pages of the book until she came to Black Magic.
>
> She explained that the woman and the panther were merely two aspects of self – the personal and the impersonal, or, for those who preferred it, conscious and unconscious.

But Norton's explanations weren't enough to keep her out of trouble this time. She was charged and found guilty of obscenity. Her book was put on a customs ban and she was fined £5. The media storm surrounding *The Art of Rosaleen Norton* put the artist at the centre of her very own 'Satanic Panic'.

In the years following her obscenity conviction, the media was abuzz with stories of a satanic cult operating out of Kings Cross – with Norton as High Priestess. The *Australasian Post* ran the headline: 'A warning to Australia: DEVIL WORSHIP HERE!' The report featured a photo of Norton wearing a pagan mask, sitting beside an altar to the god Pan. *The Daily News* published a piece titled: 'SEX WORSHIP PART OF KING'S CROSS CULT' on 24 September 1955. It claimed that 'hundreds of people are clamouring to join a weird witch cult operating at King's Cross'. According to police, the cult 'worshipped sex' and 'took drugs during rituals': 'A reporter was told today that during rituals a naked girl is placed before an altar and a live rooster is slain over her. As the blood pours over the girl's body the devotees touch the blood and chant rites.'

Thirty-seven-year-old Norton didn't reveal any of the group's practices but told *The Daily News* that 'so many people are trying to join the cult we've had to fight them off'. She admitted that the group took 'drugs and herbs as stimulants', but claimed the substances were legal.

A week later, Norton's flat was raided by police and she was charged with committing 'an unnatural sexual act'. The evidence was a series of photographs showing Gavin Greenlees, dressed in ritual apparel, spanking Norton on the bottom. (These were joke photos taken at Norton's birthday party.) The police 'witch hunt' also extended to fans of Norton's artwork. The proprietor of a Kings Cross restaurant was successfully prosecuted for publicly displaying her paintings.

Norton was also embroiled in a scandal surrounding Sir Eugene Goossens, director of the New South Wales State Conservatorium and chief conductor of the ABC's Sydney Symphony Orchestra. Goossens became involved in Norton's 'sex cult' in the early 1950s after reading *The Art of Rosaleen Norton*. The police learned of Goossens's participation in the cult when they came into possession of letters he had sent to Norton (which were stolen from Norton's flat by a tabloid journalist). On 9 March 1956, Goossens was detained by customs officials at Sydney Airport, who discovered a cornucopia of 'pornographic' material in his luggage, including approximately 1000 illicit photographs. Goossens pled guilty to possession of pornography and was fined £100 (equivalent to A$4000). The media had a field day when Goossens' relationship with Norton came to light. The celebrated conductor lost his positions and returned to England in disgrace. Meanwhile, Norton kept being 'the witch of Kings Cross'.

Norton passed away from colon cancer in 1979. She died in obscurity, having never received the artistic recognition she deserved. To the very end, she maintained her dedication to living life on her own terms. Her final words were: 'I came into the world bravely; I'll go out bravely.'

THE BOLD AND THE NOT-SO-BEAUTIFUL

O N 18 August 1984, punters at Brisbane's Eagle Farm Racecourse got to witness one of the biggest and most ridiculous scandals in Australian racecourse history. It was a day that would live in infamy, and hilarity, for decades to come. It was the day of the 'Fine Cotton affair'.

It all began in 1982, when horse breeder, bloodstock agent and con artist John 'The Phantom' Gillespie met horse trainer Hayden Haitana. The pair plotted to make a lot of money by rigging a race through a horse substitution scheme. The plan was simple:

1. Buy a horse that's good at racing.
2. Buy a horse that's not very good at racing.
3. Ensure the not-very-good horse loses multiple races, thus significantly lowering the odds of them winning.
4. Substitute the not-very-good horse for the good horse.
5. Win lots of money by betting on the not-very-good horse that should lose, but is sure to win, because it's a completely different horse.

In 1984, Gillespie bought a good racehorse named Dashing Solitaire and a not-very-good horse named Fine Cotton. The horses were worlds apart in racing ability but looked very similar, which is exactly what Gillespie wanted.

Haitana trained Fine Cotton to suck at racing, which he did. He lost every single race he entered in 1984, and the odds of him winning plummeted. Meanwhile, Gillespie clued up punters in the Brisbane crime scene that 'Fine Cotton' was a sure thing for the 18 August race. (He presumably arranged to get kickbacks from their winnings.) Everything was going according to plan until Dashing Solitaire got spooked by a kangaroo and injured himself on a barbed wire fence. Their substitution horse was out of action.

Gillespie knew it was too late to back out of the plan. Some very shady people were set to place a lot of money on Fine Cotton, and these weren't the kind of people you wanted to disappoint. Haitana suggested they amp Fine Cotton up on amphetamines to give him a 'head start'. Gillespie thought that was too risky and came up with a different scheme. They would replace Fine Cotton with a skilled racehorse named Bold Personality. The only issue was that Bold Personality looked nothing like Fine Cotton.

'It's the wrong fuckin' colour,' said Haitana. 'Fine Cotton is almost black. Bold Personality is brown ...'

Gillespie had a solution. When Bold Personality arrived from Coffs Harbour, they covered the poor creature in black Clairol hair dye. Human hair dye doesn't work that well on horses, and Bold Personality's coat turned a shade of orange. They also used a can of white spray paint to decorate the horse's legs with similar markings to the ones on Fine Cotton's legs. But by all accounts, it wasn't the most convincing effort. Strangely enough, racing stewards weren't bothered by 'Fine Cotton's' blotchy tan job and let him race.

But suspicions were aroused when a significant number of people started placing bets on Fine Cotton. The odds of him winning opened at 33–1 but dropped to 7–2 equal favourite as bets rolled in from across the country. (Queensland Police Commissioner Terence Lewis had heard the rumours about Fine Cotton and sent his mother to the racecourse to have a flutter.) The odds were very odd.

Officials knew they had to investigate when 'Fine Cotton' showed a dramatic improvement in ability and won the race by a nose. It didn't take long for them to uncover the fraud – the paint dripping off Bold Personality's leg was a bit of a giveaway. 'Fine Cotton' was disqualified and the race was awarded to the runner-up, Harbour Gold.

Gillespie and Haitana were sent to prison and given lifetime bans from horseracing. But in May 2010, Gillespie told *The Sunday Mail* that there was another side to the story. He said that 'Fine Cotton' was always supposed to lose and he'd won almost $2 million by betting on Harbour Gold. Gillespie claimed he was the mastermind behind a brilliant 'double sting' and had fooled everyone into believing the 'Fine Cotton affair' was a screw-up.

'I don't mind if people think it was a joke or whatever because I walked away with $1.8 million,' he said.

But many questioned the validity of Gillespie's story, including former Sydney race stewards chairperson John Schreck. 'With great respect to Mr Gillespie,' he said, 'anything he says you would have to take with a great big pinch of salt.'

You should probably take it with a smattering of paint as well.

EPILOGUE: THEY JUST KEEP COMING

O N 22 D ECEMBER 2023, a barnacle-covered plastic package was found on a beach in Magenta, north of Sydney. The package was full of cocaine. This was the first of many cocaine-filled packages to wash up in the following weeks. Police desperately struggled to manage the incoming tide as hundreds of kilos of blow were discovered along the NSW coastline. The cops warned the public against launching search parties or keeping any packages for themselves. (I'd hazard a guess that a few packages never made it into police custody.)

As of writing, the case hasn't been cracked, although police believe the cocaine was on a shipment from South America. 'We know syndicates will use a number of methods through shipping containers,' Detective Chief Inspector Weinstein told *ABC News*. 'Sometimes we do see where items are deliberately tossed into the ocean to be picked up by another vessel.'

Obviously something went awry, as it so often does in the world of crime. There was no doubt a criminal somewhere who miscalculated, messed up or masterminded a monumental mistake because that's what people do. Human nature dictates that there will always be a steady stream of absurd offences and foolish felonies – an assaulted Easter bunny, an abducted echidna, a posted parcel of meth, a stolen sex doll or an armed criminal who wants advice from his mum. I guess that's the wonderful thing about bizarre crime stories – they keep coming in like packages of cocaine lost at sea. Just when you think you've found them all, there's another one there, waiting to be enjoyed.

ACKNOWLEDGEMENTS

T HANK YOU, ROSEMARY MOORE. I couldn't have done this without you. If you need help burying a body, I'm your man.

Big thanks to my partners in crime: Anna Achia, Mic Looby, Julie Poulter, Cath Tavatgis and Paul Tavatgis. Your feedback and research were invaluable. If you need bail money or a character witness, call me.

Thanks to Kelly Doust for recommending me and Martin Hughes for recruiting me. Thanks to Gabriella Sterio for the thoughtful copy-edits and fact-checking. Thanks to Laura Franks for the brilliant suggestions and kind encouragement. Thanks to Josh Durham for the iconic cover and Dana Anderson for being amazing (as always). Thank you to the whole Affirm Press team. You're the ultimate caper crew.

You can't write a book (or rob a bank) on your own. Love and gratitude to Charlie Athanassiou, Natasha Brennan, Sandi Coleman, Matt Fowles, Matthew Giulieri, Carol Hagan, Simon Hendel, Jess Ho, Nicola Hogan, Ben Holgate, Campbell Mattinson, Emily Steinbach and Adam Watson.

Thank you, Denise Parsons. I look forward to writing a true crime book about you one day. In the meantime, this one's for you.

Finally, all my love to my husband, Mike. I'm proud to be the Debbie Jellinsky to your Fester Addams.